God's Fingerprints

Dusting for the Divine in the life
of a Christian Scientist Journalist

D1566581

David Horn

Hawthorne Publishing

Cover Photo: In the 1960s, when David Horn worked for The Mother Church as a watchman, only members could attend the church's annual
meeting each June. Thousands waited patiently in line for the doors to open.
That large edifice usually filled in fifteen minutes.
This rare photo, taken by an unknown photographer, was in the collection of a representative of the Christian Science Church in Indianapolis.

Hawthorne Publishing
Winds of Change Division
15601 Oak Road
Carmel, In 46033
   www.hawthornepub.com
317-867-5183

TO EVELYN

Whose devotion through the years deserves a greater tribute.

Acknowledgments

Special thanks to Jef Gibson, who patiently proofread my original text, verifying many details and correcting grammatical errors. Jef holds a Ph.D. from Cornell University and later served as a director of executive communications at the Digital Equipment Corporation.

I'm grateful to Cheryl Moneyhun, Curator of Collections at the Longyear Museum in Chestnut Hill, Massachusetts, for permission to publish the museum's historic photo of my friend Frances Thatcher, who served as a housekeeper in Mary Baker Eddy's home from 1908 until 1910.

Finally, I have nothing but good to say about Hawthorne Publishing, where Nancy and Art Baxter encouraged me to dust my life for God's fingerprints, and shepherded this book to fruition.

Publishing Editor's Note The terminology of Christian Science, like that of many religious groups, is a result of long tradition. The AP style sheet has been used in general in this book, but traditional capitalizations of parts of the church, official titles and committees and the like have been left in an older form. All photos are from the author's personal collection unless otherwise indicated.

Preface

Boston's North Station was December chilly the morning I hurried onto a commuter train bound for Rockport, Massachusetts. I longed to escape the noisy city for a quiet day of Christmas shopping in the antique seaside village, and maybe a cup of fresh clam chowder.

"Tickets, please!" the conductor shouted curtly as he strode down the aisle. Lights were dim and most windows were frosted, so everyone settled into self-absorption. We rode in silence until we reached Manchester-by-the-Sea, where a lady came aboard and took the seat beside me, all aglow. "This is my first trip to New England," she confided, "and I can't wait to go Christmas shopping in Boston."

I didn't want to burst her bubble, but there was no choice. As gently as possible I explained she'd boarded the wrong train. "You want the southbound train to the city." She blushed. She'd assumed this train was southbound, and felt foolish. What could she do? As the conductor punched her ticket, she explained her problem, but he offered no hope. "You'll have to stay aboard for our return trip to Boston this afternoon. Next time, be more careful," he muttered and then shouted "Next stop, Gloucester," as the coach door slammed behind him.

In sad silence, I listened to the rhythmic clickety-clack of the wheels as we rolled toward Cape Ann's scrub pine landscape. Suddenly the train jolted, lights flickered and we slowed down. No station was near, so we assumed something must be blocking the track ahead.

Moments later the southbound commuter to Boston inched past us in slow motion on the parallel track, and then both trains stopped side by side.

"Where's the lady who wants to go to Boston? Hurry up now!" yelled the conductor impatiently. My seatmate burst into tears as she rushed forward. Taking her arm, he helped her down three steps to the gravel median, where a conductor from the southbound train was waiting to help her aboard. Seconds later, both trains tooted their whistles and moved apart, and our coach, so long silent, filled with laughter and smiles. My seatmate's good fortune made us all friends, and it felt like Christmas. The grouchy conductor leaned through the coach door one more time. "Next stop, Gloucester," he said with a wink, "and this time I really mean it."

In our hearts, we knew the train was a metaphor for daily life. Someone who mistakenly went the wrong way was unexpectedly set right, and all who saw it felt grateful. If you dusted that train for God's fingerprints, you'd find them everywhere, especially on the brusque conductor.

In many ways, daily life resembles a train journey where we all have one-way tickets. Some seats face forward, while others face backward. In the greenness of youth, we like to go forward. We might even lean out the window, with the wind in our hair— squinting to see as far ahead as possible. Stations along the way are alluring. "Next stop, marriage! Next stop, parenthood!" calls the conductor, and the view is a blur of activity. Future plans rush rapidly toward us, only to be overtaken by newer expectations. But after the train crests the hill called middle age, our fascination with the future begins to fade. The conductor calls out stations suggesting the end of the line is near. "Next stop, Social Security. Change here for Medicare and assisted living."

By now, most of us have moved to seats facing backward, and the pace feels slower. The rush of oncoming events is behind us, and look! We can glimpse the fruit of our labor as it fades into the distance. We see how the kids turned out, and how many of our youthful hopes and dreams came true. But that's not all. With the benefit of hindsight, we can clearly see God's fingerprints on many aspects of our life—incidents of protection and guidance too wonderful to be luck or coincidence.

For the lady hoping to shop in Boston, the train ride was almost a misfortune, hard to forget. But touched by God's hand, it became a blessing she'd always remember.

Many would agree that, if there is a God, He touches the lives of special people like Gandhi or Mother Theresa or Billy Graham, probably because they have lots of faith. But what about ordinary folks like you and me? We aren't always faithful. Admit it. Sometimes we wonder if God exists. Do we receive the same care and attention He gives true believers? If my life is any measure, the answer might be "yes." I wasn't born with a silver spoon in my mouth. My parents loved me, but we were poor. Mom and Dad both worked, so I was a latchkey kid wearing hand-me-downs. I wasn't even athletic. When classmates picked teams at recess, I was usually chosen last. But my folks had faith. They never missed a service at the local Christian Science church, and took me to Sunday school. One Sunday after I acted up in class, Dad sent me to bed without lunch. I thought I'd starve, but I learned to behave respectfully in church.

With so much on His plate, could God be bothered with an unpromising kid like me? All I remember is what actually happened. You decide if it was sheer good luck, or proof of God's fingerprints.

"I have not hid thy righteousness within my heart; I have declared thy faithfulness and thy salvation: I have not concealed thy lovingkindness and thy truth from the great congregation." Ps. 40:10

1

An angel named Mrs. B

*H*er name was Lavinia L. Butterworth, but my folks called her "Mrs. B." When Mom was a teenager, Mrs. B was her Sunday school teacher. Later Mrs. B became a practitioner and teacher of Christian Science, someone who helps others solve life's problems through prayer. When Mom became pregnant with me, she told Mrs. B she feared going to the hospital, since she'd never been inside one. Mrs. B reminded her the word hospital has the same root as hospitality, and its only purpose is to help folks feel better. A few months later, I was born at Temple University Hospital, an auspicious place to begin life, since it was founded by a child's faith.

The hospital owes its existence to a little girl named Hattie May Wiatt who, in 1882, lived near Philadelphia's Grace Baptist (Temple) church, then pastored by Reverend Russell Conwell. One Sunday Conwell visited the Sabbath school and found children, including Hattie May, waiting outside because the room was full. Hoisting her on his shoulders, he carried her in and placed her on a chair, promising the church would have a bigger Sunday school when funds were available to build it. He didn't hear from her again until receiving news that she was very ill. She was only seven, and he prayed as he walked to her house, but she had died. Her parents gave him a tiny sack containing 57 cents she'd gathered to help expand the Sunday school. After preaching about Hattie's faith, he converted the coins to pennies and sold them to church members, raising $250—enough to buy the house beside the church for an enlarged Sunday school. Most donors returned their pennies, so Conwell framed and exhibited them. When the church's new Sunday school became overcrowded, members organized the Wiatt

Mite Society, using the influence of Hattie's first deposit to finance construction in 1891 of The Baptist Temple, the largest Protestant church in the United States at that time, seating 4,600 worshippers.

Conwell converted the Sunday school Hattie helped finance into a classroom for several dozen laborers he tutored at night. This grew quickly into Temple College and eventually became Temple University, including the hospital where I was born. If those original 57 pennies were dusted, each would have traces of holy fingerprints, which accounts for their infinite value.

Before I was born, Mom didn't have a clothes washer. They were scarce during World War II since metal was needed for defense. It would take a miracle to get one, and after I began using diapers she prayed for that miracle. Before long, a kind neighbor offered an old wringer washer from his garage. She still hung my diapers on the line to dry, but the machine did the dirty work. Meanwhile Dad supported the war effort by helping build Navy cruisers and submarines at Cramp Shipyard in Philadelphia. He knew Mrs. B's prayers relieved Mom's fear of hospitals, so he asked her to pray for him after an injury at work. He had accidentally glanced straight at a welder's arc, and that night was wakened by sharp pain in both eyes. Unable to open them, he asked Mom to call Mrs. B and request prayerful help. Mrs. B instructed him to return to bed and exclude everything but God from his thought, while she prayed. Within minutes he felt his eyes relax. The swelling left and the pain stopped. The next morning his eyes were fine.

After that healing, my parents drove from our modest bungalow in Wilmington, Delaware, to Philadelphia several times a year to visit Mrs. B. For some reason the ride always gave me a headache. But I didn't worry, because every time we arrived at her (to me) palatial home on West Upsal Street, she'd open the door, give me a hug, and my headache would vanish. She'd talk with Mom and Dad in the living room while Mr. Butterworth (a college professor) took me upstairs to his study, told me stories, and let me play with his huge revolving world globe. It was mounted on an oak floor stand.

Because prayer had already helped them in so many ways, Mom and Dad called Mrs. B again when I was ill in fourth grade. For some reason, I became very afraid after throwing up. I was so afraid I'd throw up again that I lost my appetite and stopped eating. I'd sip water now and then, but nothing else appealed to me. Mrs. B prayed each day, but I refused all food. I'd always been wiry, and after a week I was almost a skeleton, barely strong enough to hold a glass of water. I remember tears in Mom's eyes as she urged me to eat something. When a colleague asked Dad "How's your boy doing?" he replied, "It looks like we might lose him." Finally Mrs. B spoke with me on the phone. I remember her question. "David, what do you want me to do?" Weakly I answered, "I want you to know every truth you know." A few minutes later, Mom left the house to take a walk, defeated and hopeless. As I lay quietly in bed, I suddenly felt very hungry, so I walked to the living room and asked Dad for a sardine sandwich! He said that's not a good way to get started, and made me tomato soup instead, and after a few weeks of normal eating, I regained normal weight and returned to school. At the time, I had no clue what happened, but looking back, I think there were traces of God's fingerprints on that telephone.

When I was young, my parents were active members of First Church of Christ, Scientist, Wilmington, Delaware, a two-story Palladian-style limestone edifice with somber columns in front. Dad was head usher and served every Tuesday night in the downtown Reading Room. Mom was appointed Treasurer and later elected Second Reader. I hung out downstairs in the Sunday school, where many sessions were eminently forgettable. The most interesting class involved memorizing books of the Bible. Each student memorized five more books each week—just the titles, not the content—hoping to someday become a human Bible index. It seems unnecessary in an age of e-books, but whenever I open a paper Bible today, it's nice to know Zephaniah is in the Old Testament. I still can't find Haggai.

What made our church unique was a little old lady who served in the nursery, caring for babies and toddlers. Her name was Frances Thatcher. Like Mrs. B, she was a Christian Science practitioner, but with a difference. As a young woman, from 1908 until 1910, Frances was a housekeeper in the home of Mary Baker Eddy, founder of the Christian Science Church. She was there the day the first issue of the Christian Science Monitor was published. A bundle of papers arrived at Mrs. Eddy's home in Chestnut Hill, Massachusetts, and each staff member received one. Frances had her Monitor bound in leather and donated it to our Reading Room, where it rested for decades on a dark mahogany table.

But she donated much more than the newspaper. If prompted even slightly, she'd tell boys and girls in Sunday school about her adventures working in Mrs. Eddy's home. She liked to recall how frustrated she felt the first few weeks she was there. Mrs. Eddy took a drive in her carriage each afternoon, and staff tried to clean the house while she was out. Frances used the carpet sweeper to clean the rugs. She dusted tabletops and knick-knacks, and emptied wastebaskets, day after day after day. Some housekeepers who found the routine tiresome packed up and left, but she yearned to be useful. Finally she asked a senior staff member, "When will I be allowed to do holy work for Mrs. Eddy, instead of just homely work?" She never forgot his reply. He explained that the only differences between the words holy and homely are the letters ME. He said, "When you gain a spiritual understanding of "me," then whatever work you do will become holy."

Frances took his advice to heart. She prayed to understand who she was in the eyes of God. From the Bible she knew God is love, and she was created in God's likeness. Since God knows everything, she included all right ideas. She cherished these concepts of "me" as her true identity, and no longer felt under-utilized. She began to enjoy her work and do it gratefully. Others noticed the difference, and before long she received a promotion. She joined an elite group of household staff allowed to open the front door when the bell rang. "It may not seem like much of a promotion," she laughed, "but Mrs. Eddy was very famous, and you never knew who might be outside the door. It helped to know the nature of true identity before letting anyone in."

Nineteen-fifty-three was a red-letter year for the world, and for me. Princess Elizabeth was crowned Queen of England. Texas Instruments invented the transistor radio, and as I prepared to finish fifth grade, Mrs. B gave me the best gift any boy could wish for.

Money was tighter than usual that year. Dad's vending machine business wasn't earning much, and Mom's income as a secretary was needed to pay the bills. Who would take care of me during summer vacation from school? As usual, Mom called Mrs. B for prayerful help, but this time Mrs. B did more than pray. She asked my folks to obtain brochures from three east coast summer camps for kids who attend the Christian Science Sunday school—Camp Owatonna in Maine, and camps Crystal Lake and Elektor in Pennsylvania. She said I should be shown the brochures, but "don't influence David in any way." When I picked my favorite, she promised to pay all expenses, including tuition, uniforms, equipment, transportation, even the cost of a fishing rod, but only on one condition. I must never know of her gift. She had an unusual theory to justify this condition. From experience she'd learned that if she gave someone a gift, they usually felt obliged to pay it back, and often did. But if she gave an anonymous gift, the recipient was free of obligation, and could not repay her. That opened the door for God to compensate her generosity in holy, unexpected ways. That's why most of her charitable deeds were done in secret.

In each brochure I found pictures of kids swimming in lakes, sitting around council fires, and playing sports. No camp looked attractive to me, but Camp Elektor was the least scary. So Dad submitted an application and I was enrolled for the shortest session, one month. I later learned a month of camp cost $250. That's $2,198 in current dollars. Mrs. B paid not just for one summer, but several summers. After three years, I begged to stay at camp the entire season —two months. My folks agreed, and she secretly paid the double cost until I earned my way as a junior counselor. Her unselfish gift transformed my life forever because, like Temple University Hospital, Camp Elektor was born from childlike faith.

Hattie May Wiatt saved 57 cents to buy a building which later grew into Temple University in Philadelphia.

The former home of Lavinia L. Butterworth, CSB. Headaches I felt during the drive to visit her always vanished when I walked in the front door.

Frances Thatcher (middle, left) on the back steps of Mrs. Eddy's Chestnut Hill home, where she served as a housekeeper from 1908 until Mrs. Eddy's death in1910. Courtesy Longyear Foundation.

2

On the shores of Teedyuskung

Whether a man accepts from Fortune her spade and will look downward and dig, or from Aspiration her axe and cord, and will scale the ice, the one and only success which it is his to command is to bring to his work a mighty heart." These words by former Supreme Court Justice Oliver Wendell Holmes, Jr., were never intended to describe the life of Maude B. Clarke, but they do.

Coincidentally Holmes sat on the Court from 1905 until 1935, the same years Maude Clarke's husband left her, and she became a single Mom. She and her baby stayed with friends and guarded every penny, but eventually she had only five dollars left in the bank. There was no safety net in those days, no welfare or social security, so she prayed for a way to survive. Then she listened with childlike faith. God told her if she used her last five dollars to help others (as Hattie May Wiatt used her 57 cents), He would multiply the dollars into a lifetime income!

Educated as a teacher, Maude took a risk. She rented a room, purchased paper and crayons, and opened a nursery with her daughter as her only pupil. Soon friends sent their infants to her, and the Sunshine School was born. During Holmes' years on the bench, "Aunt Maude" grew her one-room daycare into a prosperous K-12 private school on Long Island. When older students felt the name "Sunshine School" was too childish, she allowed them to re-name the school, provided that the name included the concept of sunshine. Students discovered that the Greek word for beaming sun was "Elektor" and re-named the school Elektor Academy. The year the famous jurist (whose quote so justly applied to her) retired, in the trench of the Great Depression, she marked her 50th birthday by opening a new summer enterprise called Camp Elektor. Campers could now "let their light so shine!" For the next 30 years she and her co-director, Ardis Dunn, molded Elektor into a model of moral education, using meager profits to improve their investment in children. Even after retiring from camp at 80, Aunt Maude retained the soul of a teacher. Living with her adult daughter in Cold Spring Harbor, New York, she spent her final six years patiently teaching residents of a nearby home for the blind how to knit and crochet.

It was to this camp that I would be coming, thanks to the amazing anonymous gift. Located in the scenic Pocono Mountains of Pennsylvania from 1935 until 1970, Elektor stood on eastern shore of Lake Teedyuskung, ten miles from the village of Hawley. College-age counselors aided by twelve junior counselors supervised 70 boys and girls from six to fifteen years old. Most campers returned year after year, and there was a waiting list.

Campers awoke to the sound of reveille at 7:30 each morning. Breakfast at 8:00 was followed by cabin clean up and quiet time to study the weekly Bible lesson using citations from The Christian Science Quarterly magazine. Around 9:00 everyone assembled to sing a hymn and repeat the Lord's Prayer, and each cabin group recited a sentence memorized from the Bible lesson. Ambitious cabins could earn extra credit by memorizing and repeating a longer "special thought" like the 23rd Psalm.

After three periods of instruction in archery, riflery, tennis, baseball, rowing, canoeing, sailing, arts and crafts or swimming, the bugler blew "soupie" at noon, calling everyone to lunch in the Main House. Campers who did not like the food obeyed Aunt Maude's rule—"Three bites with no comment." After lunch, rest hour was a good time to write letters home. These were required as admission tickets for supper each Sunday.

After rest hour, we rushed from our bunks at 2:00 p.m. for special events like an all-camp soccer game or waterfront festival. Boys and girls welcomed daily "free time" from 4:00 until 5:00 when they could hang out with friends, reserve the tennis court, or sing around the upright piano in the recreation hall before supper. Evenings activities were predictable. Each Tuesday counselors unpacked the reel-to-reel projector and showed rented movies (some in color). Wednesday was church night. After a counselor read from the Bible and "Science and Health with Key to the Scriptures" by Mary Baker Eddy, campers told how prayer had helped them that week. One Saturday night each month featured a social dance hosted by the senior boys or girls, and at lakeside Vespers each Sunday, individual campers recited entire Bible stories from memory before each cabin selected a hymn for all to sing. Six-year-old junior campers always requested "Onward Christian Soldiers," and sang with gusto.

When the bugler sounded taps at 9 p.m., flashlights were turned off and light from a thousand stars filtered through the leafy forest canopy, leaving a pale glow on each quiet cabin and tent. But the lamp in Aunt Maude's upstairs bedroom in the Main House remained lit until midnight as she prayed for fresh ways to instill the shining spirit of Elektor in each camper's heart.

Her incentive system rewarded not only skill and service, but also honor. Justice Holmes could have been speaking for her when he said, "While we…do not pretend to undervalue the worldly rewards of ambition, we have seen with our own eyes, beyond and above the gold fields, the snowy heights of honor, and it is for us to bear the report to those who come after us."

The spirit of Elektor—skill, service, and honor, meant nothing to me as a 10-year-old new camper in 1953, but I did know the value of a good prank, so one day I stirred pepper into the peanut butter on our lunch table. Aunt Maude owned the camp and the peanut butter, and was told of my prank. During rest hour she summoned me to her room. I felt nervous climbing the squeaky wooden stairs in the old, unheated house. I'd never been upstairs before, and most campers considered her room the court of last resort, because she had the power to send you home. Her room was light yellow, with inexpensive flowered curtains, well-worn furniture and a small tired rug beside the bed. As I entered, she was seated across from the door in a wicker chair. I didn't know she was nearly 70, but she looked frail in her light-weight summer dress. She stared at me as I approached, and she was frowning.

"Don't you know it's wrong to waste food that's prepared with love?" she asked sharply. I nodded, feeling truly sorry. "Do you understand what the spirit of Elektor means?" I nodded again, but had no idea what she was talking about, and she read the confusion in my downcast eyes. "Here's your punishment," she announced. "I need someone to set a good example for our youngest campers this summer. Will you do that for me?" Relieved not to be sent home, I promised to do my best, and then she played her trump card.

Reaching out with both arms, she beckoned me closer until she was able to embrace me in a tight hug. "I know you'll do a good job, dear," she said in my ear, before sending me on my way.

Climbing down the stairs, I was a changed boy. Aunt Maude should have been angry, but instead she needed me. She was sure I'd do a good job! From that moment on, I belonged to her. Any camper who wanted to cross her would have to cross me first. That was the day I joined hundreds of other campers who felt the spirit of Elektor.

But Aunt Maude's kindness didn't solve my deeper problem. Each day, during free time, I sat on the fence staring down the road my folks took when they left me behind. I knew they wouldn't return for a month, but kept an eye on the road anyway, just hoping. I never told anyone why, because homesickness is like stolen candy. It's something I knew I shouldn't have, and it had weighed me down from the moment we packed my trunk at home. I'd hidden my feelings during the drive to camp. As we climbed the final miles, Mom had admired the fern-carpeted forest and Dad sniffed the pine-scented air, while I sat in back, dreading what lay ahead. We'd cruised into camp and parked in the pine grove. Five cabin mates I didn't know yet had helped unload the car. I'd gotten a handshake from Dad and a kiss from Mom, and then they'd driven away, leaving me behind.

Homesickness isn't about where you are. It's about where you aren't. At camp I learned to swim and square dance and sit Indian style around roaring council fires. And this first year I'd learned about not putting pepper in the peanut butter. But I never stopped counting the days. It was the same the second year. After I missed home for two summers, my folks begged me to return one final time. "Three strikes and you're out," Dad promised, but my homesickness vanished forever in 1955. That was the summer of Diane.

Diane reached camp on August 18, and nobody expected her since she was supposed to go to Pittsburgh. Soon after her arrival, cesspools overflowed and the sailboat capsized. She was no ordinary girl. She was the first "billion dollar" hurricane in United States history, blamed for 191 deaths, including 113 in Pennsylvania. She dropped 12 inches of rain on the Poconos, and summer resorts were especially vulnerable. At Camp Davis near Stroudsburg, 37 campers tried to escape the rising waters of Broadhead Creek by climbing into the attic of their clubhouse. They lit candles, prayed and sang hymns until a 30-foot wave swept the entire building downstream, leaving only the stone foundation and dire results for those in the attic.

Meanwhile, at Elektor, Lake Teedyuskung rose four feet, setting our wooden docks afloat. My cabin mates and I lived in an eight-man Army tent on a raised wooden platform. We lashed the flaps tightly shut and never touched the inside of the canvas with our fingers, to avoid triggering a permanent leak. Outside was windy and wet. Inside was warm and dry. After counselors gave up planning indoor activities, we sat on our bunks for hours playing cards and talking. We weren't bored or scared.

Earlier that month, Aunt Maude noticed a sale on chipped beef at the A&P in Hawley. Never one to ignore a bargain, she bought enough to feed us all for a week, and it almost did. Who knew there were so many ways to prepare and serve chipped beef?

When nature called, we'd wrap up in a poncho and splash to the Old Brown John, Elektor's only remaining out-house. I'd passed it often, but never opened the creaky door before. It was dark and cobwebbed inside, and noisy as rain pounded the corrugated tin roof, but it worked fine.

Several days into the storm, with Diane at her wild-est, a truck from a nearby general store splashed down the driveway, and we heard the bugle call "assembly." Everyone slogged to the Main House where we were greeted by huge dishes of soft ice cream on each dining table.

"My freezers are off," said the grocer, "so you kids may as well eat this before it melts." Most agreed it was the best ice cream we ever tasted.

As the storm abated, Operation Kidlift dispatched four-teen military helicopters to summer camps along the Dela-ware River. They rescued almost 600 Boy Scouts, Girl Scouts and Campfire Girls. One chopper landed on our baseball field, and officers were surprised to find no injuries; no food shortage, and no serious damage. No one dusted for God's fingerprints, but they must have been everywhere.

Did Diane ruin our summer? She certainly wrought hav-oc on the eastern seaboard, but at camp her deluge watered flowers of affection that would grow into lifelong friend-ships, and in the end, she washed away my homesickness.

When Dad and Mom finally arrived on the last day of camp, they were full of apologies and promised never to make me leave home again. "It must have been awful," they said, "being cut off from civilization without electricity or running water or a telephone, and with nothing to do."

"Oh no!" I fairly shouted. "You can't expect me to stay home. I've got to come back next summer. What if there's another hurricane?"

We never had another Diane, but thanks to the kindness of Mrs. B, I spent twelve summers at camp, eventually serving as the senior counselor assigned to help Aunt Maude pack when she retired.

"If I ever find time to write a book about my life, I'll call it 'The Five Dollar School,'" she told me, "because my life proves that a right idea can prosper without financial support. Some of the early years were difficult, especially during the war when counselors were called up for military service," but now, with camp running smoothly, she was ready to say farewell. "I won't return once I leave," she promised. "I don't believe in looking back." But after going home in July, she did return at the end of August to join us for her final Banquet Night, and that's a story that begs to be told.

"What's that old wooden thing?" friends sometimes ask when they notice family treasures displayed on my mantel at Christmas. A water-stained slice of birch with a rusty nail through the middle looks out of place next to bronze candlesticks and crisp green holly. But its band of dry, peeling bark, blanched by the passage of years, circled the seasons of my childhood, joining winter to summer. It's a reminder of Banquet Night at Camp Elektor.

Tightly wedged between neighboring lakeside cottages and resorts, Elektor was never an "outward bound" camp where children climb jagged cliffs and rafted on wild, white rapids. Instead, it was an "inward bound" camp, developing character through quieter lessons of skill, service and honor. Elektor, that Greek word for "beaming sun," distilled the essence of high adventure, blending it gently with the freshness of youth for 34 cameo summers.

Banquet Night, the final night of camp each summer,

was shrouded in secrecy. Five days in advance, counselors closed the recreation hall and covered the windows. New campers were curious, but nobody would explain why load after load of pine boughs and oak branches were dragged inside. Not far away, junior counselors sliced the long, straight trunk of a felled birch tree like a loaf of French bread.

When the magic night arrived, freshly scrubbed boys and girls who lined up to enter the rec hall could hardly believe their eyes. Inside, the familiar old building had become a forest glen. Walls covered with oak and fir boughs supported a ceiling of crepe paper tightly woven through a chicken wire grid to form a yellow E on a field of blue. Long dining tables spread with food also formed a giant letter E, and beside each plate lay a fresh slice of birch bearing a camper's name, with a nail through the center which held a short, sturdy candle. It was a sight not soon forgotten.

Junior counselors dressed in white served each child a turkey dinner with all the fixings. After dessert dishes were cleared and sunset glowed through lakeside windows, a few older counselors were awarded camp's highest recognition, a small felt beanie called the Gold Cap. Gold Cappers were a self-perpetuating group who elected new members each summer. They'd already earned every lesser award at camp, and lived "the spirit of Elektor." A Gold Capper was always your friend, always ready to help, and never sought recognition. Gold Caps were only worn on ceremonial occasions. After new recipients were recognized, everyone with a Gold Cap gathered by the banquet hall door. Applause faded to silence and someone blew a pitch pipe. Then the Gold Cappers sang, "Bless this house, O Lord, we pray, Make it safe by night and day. Bless the people here within, Keep them pure and free from sin. Bless us all, that we may be, Fit, O Lord, to dwell with thee."

After they were seated, Aunt Maude rose to give her farewell remarks. She always said the same thing. "Never forget the meaning of Elektor. When you go home tomorrow, let your light shine like the sun." Then came her long-awaited signal. "And now, boys and girls, light your candles."

Single file we walked the silent trail from the banquet hall to the lake, shielding our tiny flames from the gentle evening breeze. At the end of the pier, we knelt down and floated our candle on the still water, nudging it away from the dock before joining in a traditional friendship circle (right hand over left) to sing, "Candles afloat tonight, out on the lake. Symbols of love sincere, burning long and bright and clear."

Our youthful voices drifted from shore to shore, while a hundred tiny candles bobbed in the ebony water on a blanket of reflected starlight. As the bugle slowly sounded Taps, our summer ended, and another chapter of childhood closed forever.

The slabs of birch usually drifted ashore, and in the morning we all found our piece. We took it home, saved it for Christmas, and then put a new candle on the old nail. In its glimmer we saw the tan and friendly faces of summer. We could even hear Aunt Maude's parting admonition to let our light shine like the sun. But the slice of birch was more than a link to cherished yesterdays. It also pointed ahead, promising that eventually the snow would melt, trees would blossom, and Elektor would open again.

Thanks to the secret sacrifice of Mrs. B, I was able to float a dozen candles on those sparkling waters of childhood: twelve summers of memories that glow as brightly today as the fresh candle mounted bravely on my old slice of birch.

Camp Elektor closed in 1970. The woods are quiet now. The lake is still. But the spirit of Elektor remains in the hearts of campers from coast to coast. Recently a former counselor told me he had a perfect opportunity to omit income from his tax return. It was untraceable and he'd never be caught, but he listed it anyway. I asked why. He said, "Because of that darn gold cap."

In August, 1955, fellow campers and I survived Hurricane Diane in an eight man Army tent like this one. (I am on the left, striking a "West Side Story" pose.)

Ardis and Gordon Dunn, and Maude Clarke pose for a photo during Banquet Night at Camp Elektor.

Campers and staff form a friendship circle (right hand over left) at Camp Elektor.

3

The cloudiest year of my life

*I*n the spring of 1960, Dad got a job on the receiving dock of The Christian Science Publishing Society in Boston. I'd grown up in north Wilmington's modern, Mount Pleasant Special School District. It offered three tracks to graduation —academic (pre-college), business and general. My folks kept me on the academic track, hoping I might be the first in our family to go to college, but my shaky C average made that unlikely, even at the University of Delaware, which then accepted almost any state resident with a steady heartbeat.

Everything changed in the fall of 1960, when I began my senior year at Boston's English High School on Avenue Louis Pasteur. It stood almost next door to the famous Isabella Stewart Gardner Museum, and directly across the street from prestigious Boston Latin School. English High claims to be the oldest public high school in America, because it opened in 1821 when James Madison was in the White House. Education was different then. Students planning to enter the ministry or other scholarly pursuits were groomed at Boston Latin, while Boston English prepared working-class boys for careers in business, mechanics and engineering. During more than a century, these "working class" alumni included intergalactic "Star Trek" officer Leonard Nimoy; Presidential Medal of Freedom winner General Matthew Ridgeway; Nation of Islam leader Louis Farrakhan; Christian Science practitioner and teacher Bliss Knapp; American financier J.P. Morgan, and me.

But I had an advantage over these famous alums. By the time I arrived, English High had fallen on hard times. It was a deteriorating inner-city school where classrooms were lit by naked bulbs hanging on wires. The gym floor was cleaned once a year, so boys who did sit-ups turned their white T-shirts black. Insufficient seating in the basement cafeteria was remedied by placing a long wooden shelf around the room. Students unable go find a seat could put their lunch on the shelf and eat standing up, facing the wall. Truancy was so common that, in some classes, students who were never absent got an automatic C. Passing a test pushed the grade even higher.

It was the cloudiest year of my life. I wore a white shirt and black suit and tie to school every day and spoke only to teachers, who appreciated any kind word. But the cloud called English High had a silver lining. My grade point average rose dramatically. With so little competition, it was easy to get on the Dean's List, opening the previously closed door to college admission.

But which college? Dad didn't finish high school, and Mom never went to college, so they had no clue, and neither did I, until Dad took the bull by the horns. He went upstairs from the receiving dock and spoke with the Christian Science Monitor education editor, Millicent Taylor. He told her he'd like to send me to Principia, a small Illinois college for Christian Scientists, but it was much too expensive. Could she think of an alternative? She didn't pause a moment before asking, "Why not send him to the poor man's Principia?"

She explained that Blackburn College in Carlinville, Illinois, 40 miles north of Principia, was about the same size with 500 students, including a large, active Christian Science student organization. Loosely affiliated with the Presbyterian Church, Blackburn was fully accredited and tuition was low because it was the only college in the United States with a student-managed mandatory work program. Everyone had to work 15 hours a week on campus, even if your grandparent donated a library. Student managers could expel anyone who neglected his or her work assignment.

Best of all, Dad and Mom could afford the tuition, so I submitted an application and soon Blackburn's touring admissions counselor, Mary Cosner, knocked on our door. She said ordinarily my grades would disqualify me, but they had improved so much in my senior year that she'd make an exception. Dad was proud beyond words. His boy was going to college! None of his three brothers could make that claim. He and Mom attended my graduation from English High, and it felt like fingerprints from on high were on the diploma.

English High School occupied this old building on Avenue Louis Pasteur in Boston when I graduated in 1961.

𝕏𝟜

Interlude in the land of Lincoln

*C*arlinville is the seat of Macoupin County, Illinois, with a history vastly different from that of Boston. On August 1, 1858, Abraham Lincoln debated incumbent Senator Stephen Douglas near the town square. In 1870 residents financed and built the largest county courthouse in the United States, hoping their town might be the next state capitol. But Springfield got the nod, and Carlinville's "white elephant" still looms over the village. In 1917 Standard Oil opened two coal mines nearby, and hundreds of new mine workers created a housing crisis until the oil giant ordered 156 home kits from the Sears & Roebuck catalog. Delivered by rail, they were assembled on site and 152 still stand, making the nine-block Standard Addition the largest neighborhood of Sears homes in America. When I arrived in 1961, Carlinville was still a town to be reckoned with, boasting a Rexall drug store that sold Green River soda, two competing weekly newspapers, the Marvel Theater, a railroad station with trains to St. Louis and Chicago, and on the edge of town near the cornfields, a small college founded in 1837 by Reverend Gideon Blackburn.

It was called Blackburn Seminary until a full collegiate course was introduced during the Civil War, but the college didn't really prosper until Dr. William Hudson became president in 1912, staying 33 years. Soon after his election he initiated the work program and the number of applicants increased. In 1914 Blackburn drew national attention when the Pullman Company donated two railroad cars for use as student housing. After fire destroyed University Hall in 1927, including offices, classrooms, the chapel and rooms for 80 men, Dr. Hudson took to the rails again. Two Pullman parlor cars and two day coaches from Standard Oil became classrooms, offices and a library. When Dr. Hudson first came to Blackburn, institutional assets were less than $100,000. When he retired in 1945, they totaled nearly two million.

By the time I arrived, nine major campus buildings had been built by students, supervised by a professional construction manager. Along with subjects like history and American literature, undergrads gained skill as bricklayers, electricians and plumbers.

I was pleased to discover college was not as hard as my parents predicted. The Dean of Students coordinated everyone's class schedule, and the men's work manager let me wash pots in the kitchen after supper for 15 hours a week. College rules were strict. Girls had to sign into their dorm at 11 p.m. on weeknights. Alcohol was banned on campus, and nobody could own a car, but we didn't complain. We were all there for the same reason—to get higher education at moderate cost. A few faculty members held Ph.D. degrees, and one was Dr. John Forbes, a tall, lanky, red-haired Quaker Democrat with a doctorate in American Civilization from the University of Pennsylvania. He taught my political science class and his final exam was pass-fail. Memorize the Bill of Rights including punctuation. If you wrote it perfectly, you passed. Forget a comma and you failed. I spent many hours walking down dirt roads between cornfields repeating the first ten amendments to the Constitution over and over. It felt Lincolnesque, and I passed.

Blackburn's main classroom building, Hudson Hall, was attached to Clegg Chapel. Chapel attendance was mandatory each Sunday, with a few exceptions. We had no Jewish students, but Catholics couldn't worship in a Protestant chapel so they went to Mass in town, returning with a note signed by the priest saying they'd been there. Eventually even Protestants could worship in town, if a note from the pastor verified their attendance. But students from Christian Science homes had to attend services on campus, because the chaplain, even after reading church rules and procedures in the "Manual of The Mother Church," did not believe Christian Science was Christian. Then something happened that changed his mind.

Upperclassmen told me that, a few years before I arrived, a coed who was a Christian Scientist became quite ill. A Christian Science practitioner (like Mrs. B or Frances Thatcher) came down from Chicago and stayed with her in her dorm room, where they both prayed and took all their meals in private. Everyone waited with bated breath until, after a week, the student emerged perfectly well.

Soon the college chaplain asked to review the "Manual of the Mother Church" again, and this time concluded Christian Science is Christian and students could worship at the Christian Science Society in town if they brought back a note from the First Reader. By the time I arrived, there were enough Christian Scientists on campus to organize a club, a CS Organization. Recognized by the college, it was the only student group permitted to meet during the week in Clegg Chapel.

As often as possible, we Christian Scientists also walked a mile into town on Wednesday night to attend the weekly testimony meetings. They were exactly like the meetings at Camp Elektor, but without children. Looking back, none of these meetings stand out except one. It occurred during exam week. I'd been studying hard, and contracted a high fever. The floor monitor in my dorm recommended bed rest and orange juice, and even left a quart on the windowsill of my room, where it stayed cool. I survived an afternoon exam and rushed back to my dorm to collapse in bed when I realized it was Wednesday. Should I walk a mile to attend the evening meeting at the Christian Science Society, or get under the covers? The bed was very tempting, but something made me hike to church. I forget the topic of the readings, but I knew I wouldn't express gratitude that evening, since

I had nothing to be grateful for. But an aha! moment happened during silent prayer. Even though I felt ill, I could still be grateful that God is love and cares for everyone. In fact, I was thankful for that, so when the time came, I stood up and said so. As I spoke, perspiration began dripping steadily from the tip of my nose. I broke into a sweat and my undershirt got wet. It was very embarrassing, but after I finished thanking God for being love and returned to my seat, I realized the fever had broken. I felt as good as new. Our closing hymn that night was by John Greenleaf Whittier. "The healing of the seamless dress is by our beds of pain; We touch him in life's throng and press, and we are whole again." The Society hymnals were old and tattered, but on that faded page I think I saw the touch of God.

After exams were over and classes ended, I returned to Pennsylvania to be a counselor at Camp Elektor. Mom had to give up her job, and my folks didn't have enough savings to send me back to college for my junior year, but they didn't tell me. They hoped funds might become available before I had to return in the fall. During the summer I came down with a first-rate case of conjunctivitis. For days my eyes would not open in the morning until soaked with a warm washcloth. My prayers had no effect, so I called Mrs. B and asked her to pray for me. The next morning both eyes popped open easily, completely dry and healthy. But something even better happened. I awoke hearing these words clearly in thought. "True currency takes form in ideas." I wasn't sure why I felt that so strongly, until I returned home and learned money had run out and my Blackburn days were finished. Something new needed to evolve.

Hudson Hall and Clegg Chapel, built in the early 1930's by students in the work program with help from professional contractors, form the center of the Blackburn College campus. Clegg has hosted many visiting speakers, including Carl Sandburg in 1932. When I enrolled in 1961, Sunday chapel attendance was still mandatory.

5

Return to Boston

I didn't want "drop-out" on my resume as friends began their junior year of college in the fall of 1963, but with Mom unemployed, Dad needed help paying bills so I took an entry level position in the Christian Science Monitor advertising department. I began work immediately, but my heart ached for Blackburn. When I learned two former 'Burnians, Dave and Sally Anderson, were teaching at the Palmer House School near North Conway, New Hampshire, I borrowed Dad's Corvair and drove up for a surprise visit. Dave and Sally were older than I and I knew Sally through the Christian Science Org. They had graduated and were now teaching at this private school. My visit was to be more of a surprise than anyone expected.

The road from North Conway to their school in Eaton Center was curvy, and I negotiated each turn with ease until suddenly I became a poster child for a book by young lawyer Ralph Nader.

In his 1965 bestseller, "Unsafe at Any Speed," Nader accused the auto industry of resisting needed safety features like seat belts and padded dashboards, but his book is best remembered for the first chapter, "The Sporty Corvair—the One-Car Accident." Nader claimed the Corvair had a suspension defect that made it easy for the driver to lose control and roll the car over. He was correct, but I didn't know it until I swept around the final curve before reaching Palmer House School. My car lost traction on gravel and slid sideways off the road until the left front wheel dropped into a shallow rut, causing the rear end to flip high in the air behind me. Thinking "this may be your last roll," I grabbed the wheel, flicked off the ignition and crouched low against the seat as the car flipped end-over-end, flattening the roof before bouncing back onto its wheels in a field.

Shards of glass filled my pockets, but I emerged without a scratch.

I stood alone next to the wreck, and the godly fingerprints were not apparent until the only man I knew in the entire state, Dave Anderson, suddenly drove into view. He wasn't expecting me that day, but he'd seen everything that happened and gladly hitched my car to his truck and pulled it back to the school where he worked. It was a spacious Greek Revival home built in 1884, and I was welcomed to join students for a delicious seafood supper. To my relief, no one at the table asked about the smashed Corvair just outside the dining room window, and it was soon gone.

A Chevrolet body shop was not far away, and Dave promised to tow my car there the next morning, and my return trip to Boston was easily arranged. Several parents were visiting their children who boarded at the school. One dad from Rhode Island was leaving after supper and offered to drop me off in Boston on his way home. Three weeks later the body shop called to say the car was repaired. My new Rhode Island friend was returning to see his daughter again and picked me up at my door. Dave had driven the Corvair back to the school where we found it standing proudly in the driveway, better than new. Insurance covered the restoration.

Mary Baker Eddy, who founded the Christian Science church, believed accidents are unknown to God. If that's true, and if God knows everything, then did I really have an accident, even a lucky one? Or was it just another proof of God's care? Only time would tell.

When I began working in Monitor advertising that month, The Christian Science Publishing Society (CSPS) and The Mother Church (TMC) together had about 1,600 employees. Erwin (Spike) Canham was the most famous. He was the Monitor's editor from 1945 until 1974, but he wasn't the only inspiring role model. Peter Henniker-Heaton, the Monitor's much loved literary editor, taught my Sunday school class, and when he was absent, an editor of the church magazines, Ralph Wagers, filled in for him.

But strange as it seems, the employees I admired more than any others were the grandmotherly cafeteria ladies. I suspect many were widows who came to Boston to "give their life to the church." If so, they probably lived next to CSPS in tiny church-owned apartments on Clearway Street, and had cats. But they had more than cats. They also had great love. When employees hurried off three elevators at the 9th floor cafeteria each noon and lined up with trays, the ladies welcomed many by name! How well did they know us? I can't speak for others, but I usually ordered meatloaf, potato salad and coleslaw, and one afternoon when I didn't arrive until the cafeteria was closing, they assured me, "We put your favorite aside, just in case you came late."

Most students of Christian Science have heard of "the love of The Mother Church." Usually it describes how the church loves the world and its many branch churches around the world. But to me it means cafeteria ladies, and here's why.

When I worked there, each department in CSPS had a "cafeteria contact." Boston is famed for frigid winters, and around 10 a.m. each winter morning the phone would ring on each cafeteria contact's desk. Whether in accounting, advertising, the newsroom, the mailing room or the press room, the contact heard four words. "The brownies are ready."

That was a signal for the contact to stroll from desk to desk in his or her department, collecting a nickel from any-one who wanted a brownie. (Orange juice was available in vending machines.) After collecting a handful of nickels, the contact rode the elevator to the 9th floor, and soon returned with a tray of fragrant brownies, warm from the oven. One brownie on a paper napkin was placed on the desk of anyone who had paid a nickel. We never stopped working, but we savored each bite of our brownie, because it was seasoned with affection.

Years later, the cafeteria was remodeled into offices. A larger lunchroom overlooked the new reflecting pool, and catering was outsourced. But even now, I dare anyone to ride the CSPS elevator to the 9th floor on a cold winter morning at 10:00. Step into the corridor, close your eyes, be very quiet and take a deep breath. You can still smell the brownies, and feel the loved that baked them.

The Christian Science Publishing Society building, opened in 1934, included an employee cafeteria on the 9th floor where, in the mid-1960s, cooks baked brownies on cold winter mornings.

6

The Christian Science Monitor Youth Forum

*A*fter World War II, Christian Scientists noticed their children enjoying events hosted by other churches in town—churches with recreation halls where boys and girls played basketball or danced. The Christian Science church couldn't "officially" engage youth except in Sunday school, since our Church Manual is silent on social gatherings. But we had another choice. We could hitch youth activity to a star, our highly respected, prize-winning newspaper.

The first Christian Science Monitor Youth Forum for young men and women ages 16 to 30 opened in Boston in 1947, and the idea took off like wildfire. Within six years, more than 500 Youth Forums circled the globe. These Forums were usually organized by local Christian Science parents, although some began as college clubs. In 1948, for example, the Monitor Youth Forum at Kansas State College (now University) in Manhattan, Kansas, boasted 30 members. But to reach full potential, such diverse groups needed coordination.

Enter Miss Elizabeth Woolley, a youthful Christian Science practitioner and prolific contributor to church magazines. Hired by the Monitor as "Headquarters Secretary" for Youth Forums, she and her staff occupied a suite of second-floor offices in Falmouth Hall, 241 Huntington Avenue, adjacent to the original grassy park in front of The Mother Church. Built in 1901 by Chickering & Sons piano company, Falmouth Hall featured a 200-seat recital auditorium where Youth Forum events were held. With help from Forums worldwide, Miss Woolley awarded "travelship" grants to deserving members. Some young Christian Scientists saw

Europe for the first time as travelshippers, reporting their adventures in fascinating articles on the Monitor's Family Features page. In 1948, the young president of the Monitor Youth Forum in Berlin, Germany, was awarded a $250 travelship to help him attend Reed College in Portland, Oregon. His name was Arno Preller, and he later became a practitioner and teacher of Christian Science, as did one of his sons.

Typically, Youth Forum meetings began with a discussion of current news in the Monitor, followed by light refreshments and a social hour. Fellowship was a high priority, and older Sunday school students often met their future spouses at Forum meetings.

That's why many were disappointed on December 31, 1959, when the Monitor closed Forum headquarters in Boston. Individual Forums could remain active, but without "unofficial" coordination, most withered.

Members of the Boston Youth Forum inherited Miss Woolley's furnished offices and Falmouth Hall at no cost, but even with these assets, most stopped attending meetings. By January 1965, the Boston Forum had only one member left. He worked in the Monitor newsroom and hoped to quit the Forum and vacate the office as soon as anyone else showed interest in it. After we spoke briefly about future Forum possibilities, he removed the key to Falmouth Hall from his chain and handed it to me. The Boston Youth Forum was now mine—"lock, stock and barrel."

Touring the unused but well-furnished offices, I found letterhead stationery, typewriters, a mimeograph machine, even a checkbook with a $200 balance. The telephone worked, so I called four twenty-something colleagues and we formed a planning committee. If the Forum had no future, why not go out with a bang instead of a whimper? Miss Woolley attended one of our meetings to share wisdom gained during her decade as headquarters secretary.

During one planning session, a young lady on our committee (a graduate of Blackburn College) said she was just hired by the phone company and could make free long distance calls. The Annual Meeting of The Mother Church was only three months away. Back Bay Boston would be awash with church members. Should she call Alan Young in Studio City, California, and ask if he'd give a free talk to the Forum on Saturday before the meeting? We loved her idea, so she called and learned he was coming to Annual Meeting anyway, and would be honored to speak to the Forum. He'd call his talk, "The Role of a Christian Scientist in Show Business."

We had a hunch Alan Young would be a big draw, and here's why: he was playing that role himself.

Several famous actors and actresses were students of Christian Science. Ginger Rogers, Jeanne Stapleton and Georgia Engel often attended the Annual Meeting of The Mother Church. But Young was the only one who co-starred with a talking horse. His role from 1958 to 1966 as Wilbur Frost on the "Mister Ed" show made Young a household name. "Mister Ed" won a Golden Globe, and can still be seen on cable TV today.

Once Young agreed to speak, we began eager preparations. One committee member bought him a small crystal paperweight as a token of appreciation. Three others located hundreds of folding chairs and set them up for maximum seating. I went to E.D. Abbott Company, a small commercial printer at 181 Massachusetts Avenue, near CSPS, to buy printed invitations. We couldn't afford a custom engraving of Mister Ed, and hoped they might have a generic horse's head on file. They had one from the cover of the Suffolk Downs racetrack restaurant menu. It wasn't the famous TV horse, but it was free, so we put it on tri-fold invitations which were posted on all bulletin boards at TMC and CSPS, and sent to as many friends and fellow employees as possible.

A month before Annual Meeting, people were requesting handfuls of invitations to give friends. I was only an entry-level clerk in Monitor advertising, but one day a trustee of the Publishing Society called me personally from his paneled office on the 8th floor.

"How can I get an invitation to hear Alan Young's talk?" he asked. "Someone said I should call you directly." It was a heady moment for this Blackburn College drop-out.

Alan Young's talk was the best-attended event in the history of the Boston Youth Forum. Every chair was filled and people stood along the walls. He told how he'd been afflicted with asthma as a boy and was often confined to bed. After his mother became interested in Christian Science, she enrolled him in Sunday school and he had an instantaneous healing. One minute he could hardly breathe. The next minute he could breathe freely and even play soccer. As he grew up, he never made a career move without praying about it first. He gave God credit for everything he had accomplished in show business.

After that meeting, some felt the Boston Forum might have a future after all, but they were wrong. The prints of the Divine were on that meeting, but we could never replicate such success. Three years later, in 1968, Falmouth Hall was demolished to make space for the new Church Center Sunday School building.

Actor Alan Young starred in the television series "Mr. Ed." That's Connie Hines, his TV wife next to him. During this time he was a guest speaker at the Boston Youth Forum.

7

Dining at Mrs. Eddy's home

*M*ost students of Christian Science are familiar with the address 385 Commonwealth Avenue, in Boston. Church founder Mary Baker Eddy purchased this brownstone in 1887, moving in at Christmas time. Eighteen months later, after relocating to New Hampshire, she rented 385 to her students, and eventually Judge Septimus Hanna and his wife Camilla lived there. He was First Reader of The Mother Church, and Mrs. Eddy later stipulated in the Church Manual that all First Readers should occupy her home during their term in office. This was helpful because First Readers usually came from distant cities and had no Boston residence.

Back in the 1960s, the historic home was not open for tours. Unless you were a church executive or a friend of the family, you never stepped inside, so I was thrilled to be invited to 385 for supper one evening. Here's how it happened.

Readers at The Mother Church serve three-year terms, beginning at Annual Meeting. In 1962, Gordon F. Campbell of Santa Monica, California, became First Reader. His son, Gordon Campbell Jr. (Gordo), was about to graduate from Principia College. After graduation, Gordo joined his folks at 385 and found an entry level job in Monitor advertising. When I arrived in the fall of 1963, he was working at the desk beside mine. Soon we were best friends, and when he became engaged to his future wife, he asked me to be best man. I was honored to accept, and soon was invited to dinner at 385 as part of the wedding party. It was an evening to remember.

We pulled the antique bell on the front door, and Mrs.

Campbell greeted us warmly and invited us into the formal front parlor, where elegant overstuffed chairs rested on a deep rose-colored carpet, and a beautifully framed portrait of Mrs. Eddy hung above the fireplace. Rose was apparently Mrs. Eddy's favorite color, and flocked rose and white wallpaper covered the walls. A large velvet drape was drawn across the wide arch into the adjoining dining room, but after a few moments of nervous conversation the drape opened, revealing candles, candles, and more candles—all pink. Two candelabra adorned a long dining table laden with crystal stemware and china, while brass sconces on the walls added a soft glow. Mr. Campbell sat at one end of the table; Mrs. Campbell at the other, with four of the wedding party on each side.

As soon as we said grace, a door to the serving pantry opened and an elderly butler named James entered with plates of artfully arranged food. We all relaxed as we ate and chatted about the upcoming wedding. We were a laughing, happy group and after the last person finished, James magically reappeared in his black suit, white shirt and black tie to remove the plates. He quickly returned and gave each of us a small crystal bowl of water with pink rose petals floating on top. I remember thinking, "This is the strangest dessert I've ever seen, but if Mrs. Campbell eats it, I will too." Of course she didn't eat it. She dipped her fingers into it and dried them daintily on her cloth napkin. I had never used a fingerbowl before, or since. Mrs. Campbell explained, "I like to give you young people the same service I'd give the church directors if they were visiting, so you'll have the experience." Then, again as if by magic, James appeared and replaced the fingerbowls with bowls of ice cream, which was reportedly Mrs. Eddy's favorite dessert. Later I discovered why James' timing was so good. A button lay concealed beneath the carpet in front of Mrs. Campbell's dining chair. When James was needed, she simply placed her foot on the button and pressed it.

After ice cream, James brought each of us a flavorful cup of coffee. Naturally one of the wedding party questioned this, since Mrs. Eddy never served coffee in her home except to visiting workmen. "Oh don't worry," Mr. Campbell assured us. "It's decaffeinated."

When supper was finished, Mrs. Campbell took the young women to her upstairs parlor for a visit. We men joined Mr. Campbell in his study, where he revealed the modern reel-to-reel tape recorder he used to practice his Sunday readings. Finally we all toured the historic upper rooms, including the tower room and one bedroom furnished entirely by Augusta E. Stetson, a pupil of Mrs. Eddy's from New York City.

Gordo's wedding in the Boston suburb of Wellesley Hills is a blur to me now, but memories of supper at 385 are clear as crystal.

Mrs. Eddy resided at 385 Commonwealth Avenue from December, 1887, until moving to New Hampshire in June, 1889. She kept this home as a residence for the First Reader of The Mother Church.

8

The great New England blackout

*F*ive months after Alan Young spoke to a packed house at Falmouth Hall, something else happened at the Christian Science Monitor that caught everyone's attention. The lights went off.

Most Monitor employees worked from 8 a.m. until 4:15 p.m., but Christmas display ads were flooding in from many parts of the world, so I stayed late at the Overseas Desk in first floor advertising (later the site of "Quotes Café") to process them.

Winter sun sets early in Boston, and it was dusk outside at 5:21 on Tuesday, November 9, 1965, when my IBM Selectric typewriter stopped humming. One by one, overhead fluorescent lights flickered off, and outside the window, lights on Norway Street went dark. I called my parents, who lived six blocks away on Charlesgate East. Their lights were off too. We doubted all of Boston could be without power, but we were wrong.

As I grabbed my coat and strode out the front door of CSPS to meet a coworker named Dick Stratton and investigate, my girlfriend was riding on a bus to Boston from Washington, DC. As it sped north along the New Jersey Turnpike, the driver used the PA system to invite passengers to look out and see "the sparkling skyline of New York City at dusk." Everyone looked, but there was no sparkle. The driver was flummoxed. Like us, he didn't know 30 million people from the Big Apple to Niagara Falls were without power. An estimated 800,000 riders were trapped in stalled subway trains in darkened tunnels. Others were stuck on elevators. As he drove into the New York City Port Authority bus terminal, the only interior lights the driver saw were candles.

Meanwhile, back in Boston, Dick told me he'd been standing on the Massachusetts Avenue bridge over the Charles River watching students from MIT gracefully row racing shells on the water below. As one shell glided beneath the bridge, he saw its tiny light mirrored in the smooth water. When it emerged on the other side, it was the only light for miles. "From Kenmore Square to Beacon Hill, the city blinked and flickered out," he said, leaving only the shine of a full "hunter's moon."

Dick and I walked downtown, and my transistor radio became a magnet, drawing knots of curious listeners at each corner. We heard the scope of the blackout, and rumors that it may have been triggered by an alien spacecraft touching a generator near Niagara Falls to refuel.

Actually, it was caused by the tripping of a 230-kilovolt transmission line near Ontario, Canada. This caused several other heavily loaded lines to fail, breaking up the entire Northeastern transmission network. Thirty million people were in the dark.

A riot at the unlit Walpole state prison had to be suppressed with tear gas, but on the streets of Boston we saw no looting or panic. Strangers chatted amiably on sidewalks. They seemed contented, almost amused, by their plight. Restaurants offered free food before it spoiled, providing beggars with an unexpected bounty.

But motorists were another story. Without traffic signals, rush hour traffic had quickly become gridlocked. Many drivers turned off their engines is despair, expecting to go nowhere, but then as if by magic, traffic began moving again.

University students who lived in fraternity houses along busy Boston streets came outside in droves and commandeered intersections. Waving their arms to direct traffic, they coordinated their signals over several blocks. Drivers gratefully obeyed the students, and traffic picked up speed.

The New York Knicks called off their basketball game against the Boston Celtics that night, but it didn't matter.

Boston played a game against the blackout and won. Emergency generators helped hospitals survive, but in the Back Bay, the only outdoor lights that never went off were globe lamps in The Mother Church Park. Dick and I were sorry when power was restored by morning. Without electricity, strangers became friends and anything seemed possible.

9

Church security

*I*needed to finally complete my education. After a year at CSPS, I applied to the only school I could afford —Boston State College. Located within walking distance of CSPS, it served commuter students and cost $100 per semester plus books. It was fully accredited, and the degree I earned qualified me to take the Law School Admission Test in 1968 and enroll at American University's Washington College of Law.

To facilitate taking daytime classes at Boston State, I left Monitor advertising and became a watchman for The Mother Church. In recent years, church watchmen have evolved into gracious security hosts who wear matching blazers. Some ride in a golf cart, chatting casually with folks they meet on the spacious church center plaza. Remote cameras record activity at building entrances, and employees wear badges authorizing admission to upper floors of CSPS. In 1965, cutting edge technology meant carrying a walkie-talkie with a long whip antenna. We were to be as invisible as possible when we patrolled streets and alleys around church property. Our job was to watch.

Consider the manicured park in front of The Mother Church, for example. On summer nights, a watchman might be assigned to sit in a parked car along Norway Street and watch the grass. We weren't concerned that someone would steal the sod, but every now and then a young couple from one of the nearby universities would wander from campus looking for a quiet place to cuddle. The park was safe, and had several private spots where folks could relax on the grass under cover of darkness.

If we were assigned to watch the grass and saw a couple embracing under a bush or tree, our instructions were clear. Don't engage the couple. Don't explain that this is church property, or offer a free copy of the Christian Science textbook. Instead, simply activate the remote control underground lawn sprinklers. It wasn't the same as baptism, but it worked every time.

If you ever attended a service in The Mother Church, you may have wondered after the offering where the collection went. In the early 1960s, ushers brought the bags of money to a secure counting room beside one of the rear balconies. After the service, it took time to count, sort and package bills and coins from hundreds of worshippers. After it was totaled, the collection stayed in a vault in the counting room until Monday morning, when an armored truck arrived to take it to the bank.

In those days, the supervisor of church security had a pistol. He never carried it except on Monday morning, when he accompanied the Sunday collection from the counting room downstairs and out the door to the armored truck parked by the curb on Falmouth Street. This weekly procedure was uneventful and, as far as I know, the pistol was only fired once. Before the truck arrived one Monday, while the supervisor loaded the revolver in his office, he accidentally shot a hole through his filing cabinet. All the watchmen were grateful he escaped injury, but after that, he was sometimes compared to Barney Fife, the comically inept deputy sheriff of Mayberry on "The Andy Griffith Show" from 1960 to 1965.

Church security had its lighter moments, such as when two night watchmen would lie on distant pews in The Mother Church extension and play flashlight tag on the darkened dome. But there were also nights of unforgettable inspiration. I was fortunate to have one of these in 1965.

During the last years of her life, Mrs. Eddy lived in a large stone mansion at 400 Beacon Street in the Boston suburb of Chestnut Hill. It was spacious enough to accommodate her staff of 14 to 24 people. For some years it had been open to the public, and trained guides gave tours every day. But they went home at 5:00 p.m. and insurance required the building be occupied 24/7. Church security filled the gaps by providing night watchmen, and one evening the scheduled watchman called to say he needed time off in a few days. I still remember hearing the supervisor call out to the staff, "Anybody want to do 400 on Friday night?" Most felt it was boring and nobody volunteered, except me. I had toured the home, but never been there alone overnight with total freedom to wander anywhere.

The next evening I visited 400 at 7:00 p.m. to be trained by the watchman who would be absent Friday. He showed me the schedule—tour every room of the house once an hour, checking to be certain all windows and exterior doors are locked. Leave the lights off and use a flashlight. Always wear bedroom slippers to preserve the carpet. Spend any idle time in the parlor of what was called "the practitioner wing." And yes, it was okay to brew a hot beverage in the kitchen.

I arrived early that Friday. In my briefcase were a copy of the Christian Science textbook, "Science and Health with Key to the Scriptures," by Mrs. Eddy, along with a flashlight and a pair of comfy slippers.

As I made my first hourly tour of the building, I remembered my boyhood Sunday school where Frances Thatcher recalled working in this home from 1908 until 1910. The interior was preserved after Mrs. Eddy's death. Furnishings were almost all original. I walked on the same carpet Mrs. Thatcher swept 55 years earlier, when she prayed to understand the spiritual meaning of "me" until her homely work became holy. I could almost feel her presence.

My night at 400 ended at 7 a.m. in a moment of unforgettable beauty. After finishing a final tour of all the rooms, I was descending the wide staircase from Mrs. Eddy's study to the downstairs hall when I had to stop. Sunlight poured through lace curtains in the living room. The grandfather clock beside the front door filled the house with deep, rich tones as it slowly began the Westminster chimes. Standing on the stairs, I felt grateful for every trace of God's fingerprints I'd seen thus far in my life, thanks to the study of Christian Science. I didn't know what the future held, but I knew what held the future.

The parlor at Chestnut Hill in this historic photo from 1909 or 10 appears similiar to the parlor I saw when I served there overnight. The photo is reproduced in the book Mr. Dickey: Secretary to Mary Baker Eddy, Chestnut Hill Edition *by Nancy Baxter. The original taken by Dickey himself is now in the Keith McNeil collection.*

Mrs. Eddy lived at 400 Beacon Street from 1908 until her death in 1910.

Most of Mrs. Eddy's original furniture was still in the home when I served here as a substitute night watchman. While patrolling each main floor room hourly to make sure windows were locked, I remembered hearing that Mrs. Eddy enjoyed sitting at her desk at dusk to watch the sunset. Lamps in her study were turned off, and when it became dark she could not see any of the clocks on her desk. Someone built her a small wooden box containing a battery, a flashlight size lightbulb and a button. Atop the box was a small clock. When she pressed the button with her finger, the bulb illumined the face of the clock so she could tell the time. While patrolling her study, I checked her desk to see if this device was still there. It was.

Sunlight shining through the lace curtains of parlor windows inspired me in the morning as I completed a final patrol through Mrs. Eddy's Chestnut Hill home.

❦*10*

Name, rank and serial number

*D*uring the first years of the Vietnam War, draftees were a minority of U.S. armed forces, but their higher numbers in the Army meant they eventually became a majority of infantry troops, and half of Army battle casualties.

Earlier in the war, enrollment at Blackburn College shielded me from this danger, since full-time university students were exempt from the draft. But when I dropped out of college after two years, Uncle Sam took notice. Early in 1964, while working in Monitor advertising, I received a draft notice, and showed the unopened envelope to Gordo Campbell. He suggested I leave it sealed; hurry downtown to the Navy Recruiting Center, and volunteer immediately for the Naval Reserve. He said Navy chow was better than Army grub, and very few sailors fought in Vietnam. "If you go into the infantry," he warned, "be prepared to sleep in a wet foxhole."

After work that day I drove to the Fargo Building in Boston and joined the Naval Reserve. Navy recruiters called it a "midnight enlistment" since I was due to report to the Army the next morning. I returned the next day to complete paperwork for the Navy and heard Army recruiters in the next room call my name, but I didn't answer. When Navy recruiters called, I answered immediately, and since I had just enrolled full-time at Boston State, they offered me a three-year deferment from active duty to finish college. I'd have to attend drills one weekend a month and two weeks each summer, but my active duty would not begin until 1967. I felt very fortunate, and then things got better.

Back in the advertising department, Gordo suggested I request a transfer to something called the Naval Reserve Security Group. Each sailor in the Group held a top-secret cryptographic clearance, and Gordo believed enlisted personnel with top secret clearances would never see combat. After a few months of weekend drills, I requested the transfer and it was approved. For the next few months, friends reported being contacted by investigators who asked questions about me, and in due time the clearance was received. My future in the military appeared safe, and more good fortune was just around the corner.

Most new recruits endured two months of basic training at the Great Lakes Naval Training Center near Chicago. Today, it's the Navy's only recruit training center, but during the Vietnam War a smaller boot camp was open closer to Boston. I received orders to the Naval Construction Battalion Center in Davisville, Rhode Island, home of the legendary SeeBees. From WWII to Korea to Afghanistan, SeeBees built bases, airstrips, roadways and other military construction. They often lacked necessary supplies, earning the motto, "We've done so much with so little for so long, that now we can do everything with nothing forever."

At Davisville, two months of boot camp were squeezed into two weeks. We were busy every second, but chow in the SeeBee mess hall was almost gourmet.

Basic training is just what it says, basic. Drill sergeants screamed in our faces and ridiculed us as we marched in formation on the parade ground. After a few days I felt discouraged and asked to see the Protestant chaplain. He inquired about my religion, and I told him I was a student of Christian Science.

"You know the problem with Christian Scientists?" he asked. "You only read little bits of the Bible each week. You need a much bigger dose. I recommend you read the entire book of John." Well, why not? So I read the Gospel of John in my bunk each evening before lights out, and it helped me feel better.

That Sunday I attended what the Navy called Protestant Divine Worship, and heard a sermon I've never forgotten. The chaplain described an auction where folks were bidding on valuable antiques. Winning bids were high until the auctioneer held up a dusty old violin. "What am I bid?" he asked, but no hands went up. Finally someone bid five dollars; then another bid ten. The auctioneer was about to declare "sold for ten dollars" when an elderly gentleman emerged from the crowd and took the violin from the auctioneer. After carefully tuning the strings, he played part of a Beethoven sonata.

The tones were so pure that the audience listened in amazement until the old man returned the instrument and disappeared into the crowd.

"NOW what am I bid?" called the auctioneer, and many hands shot up. "One thousand." "Two thousand." Finally the violin sold for three thousand dollars.

The chaplain asked us if we knew why the later bids were so much higher? We didn't, so he told us the value was increased by the touch of the Master's hand.

"Sometimes you may feel almost worthless, especially here at boot camp," he said, "but you're not worthless. You each have enormous value, and others will recognize your value if you let yourself be touched by the Master's hand."

To close the service, everyone stood and sang the Navy hymn. Its original words were penned in England in 1860 for a young man about to sail for America, but in that modest base chapel, among raw recruits wearing "dress whites," the hymn was more of a prayer. We prayed it as we sang, "Eternal Father, strong to save, Whose arm hath bound the restless wave, Who bidd'st the mighty ocean deep its own appointed limits keep; Oh, hear us when we cry to Thee for those in peril on the sea!"

The next three years passed quickly, and graduation from Boston State College ended my deferment. Active duty would begin any day, but where would I be sent?

During the Vietnam War, every sailor serving on a ship needed three or four sailors on shore to handle his paperwork. As a weekend warrior, I'd become a desk jockey processing endless forms, since I could type 60 words a minute. Our commander felt I'd serve the Navy best as a personnel clerk or Communications Technician (CT), and when he spotted two unfilled seats in the next CT class at Bainbridge Naval Training School in Maryland, he told me about them. "These open seats won't last long," he told me. "You can have one if you want." I accepted gladly.

Bainbridge Naval Training Center, like Boston English High, was showing its age when I arrived. Built hastily in 1942, some of the temporary wooden WWII barracks were still occupied 25 years later. The nearest towns were tiny Port Deposit and Perryville, and Havre de Grace at the head of Chesapeake Bay. Sailors returning to Boston from Bainbridge told me to forget about off-base housing. There was none.

But times were changing in rural Maryland. In 1963, President John Kennedy dedicated a new 48-mile Northeastern Expressway, later known as I-95. When I approached Port Deposit on the new highway, exits were still numbered consecutively, and exit 7 was marked Bainbridge Naval Training Center.

The CT course lasted eleven weeks, and I was assigned a bunk in the barracks. But during the first weekend I did what other "white hats" did before me. I searched in vain for off-base housing. Nothing was available, and I was returning to the base when I came to a T in the road. Almost whimsically I prayed, "Father, which way should I go?" and immediately heard the words "Turn right." Neither direction appeared promising, but out of curiosity I heeded the voice and turned right. Around the next bend, within walking distance of the base, stood a three-story inn surrounded by lush green fields and orchards. The large enclosed front porch was a restaurant, and upstairs were small rooms and suites. Atop the roof, visible from the elevated expressway, tall red letters announced EXIT SEVEN MOTEL. I parked my car and noticed a tiny "Vacancy" sign by the door. The owner said vacancies were rare, but someone had just checked out an hour ago, and that man's room, the only one on the top floor under the sloping roof, was available. It had a stove, sink, tiny bathroom with triangular shower stall, and a bedroom. Views from the dormered windows were pastoral, so I registered and lived there for the next ten weeks. I never forgot the mysterious voice urging me to "Turn right." I didn't know I'd hear it again, more than once, as the years went by.

The first week of training focused on typing. Everyone had to type at least 20 words a minute to continue the course. Instruction in the use of various naval personnel forms, abbreviations, etc., began the second week with an exciting announcement.

We all knew we'd be transferred somewhere else when the course ended, and we were told it took the Pentagon nine weeks to cut orders for our next duty station. As an incentive to study hard, the instructor promised that whoever earned the highest score on the test at the end of the second week would have his choice of duty stations. In other words, he would not be sent to Vietnam unless he requested it. This offer got our total attention, and we prepared to study hard.

Late Monday afternoon of that second week, we were ordered to leave class early and receive fluoride treatment on our teeth. This was routine for trainees, but the fluoride we received was not flavored with mint. It tasted awful, and we were ordered not to rinse for an hour.

When I enlisted, I indicated my faith as "Christian Scientist." This qualified me for exemption from medical care except in an emergency. Rather than submit to a foul taste for an hour, I used the exemption to opt out, and returned to my motel room to study and retire early. My classmates were aware that I had not taken the fluoride.

When I awoke Tuesday morning, my nose was dripping like a spigot. I sneezed often and felt tired. The problem was too severe for tissues. I kept a roll of toilet paper on my desk all day, unrolling it almost constantly to blow my nose.

I was too weary to study Tuesday night and just fell into bed. On Wednesday I felt no better. I had "the mother of all head colds," and didn't know why.

Unable to regain health through my prayers, I called a Christian Science minister and asked him to visit me at my motel room Wednesday evening.

A Christian Science minister isn't really a clergyman. He or she is usually a member of a Christian Science church near a military base. If someone from the base calls the church for prayerful support, the minister responds. I'd never called one before, so I didn't know what to expect.

He arrived quickly, and opened the trunk of his car. Inside were dozens of little Bibles and matching copies of the Christian Science textbook. They were small enough to fit in a shirt pocket, and he insisted I take a set.

He could see my problem, and asked how things were going in class. I told him about the fluoride treatment, and the possibility of selecting my own duty station if I earned the highest score on the test Friday morning.

"Would you please pretend I'm a stranger to Christian Science, and just do whatever you do?" I asked. "I'm exhausted, and I need to feel well for Friday's test."

He pointed out that my fellow sailors all spent an hour with foul-tasting fluoride in their mouths, and I didn't. "Those classmates knew you were not taking this treatment. Do you think that, without meaning any harm at all, they might have thought, 'Horn is a Christian Scientist. Christian Scientists often rely on prayer instead of medicine for healing, but they all get sick sooner or later?'" I supposed they might have felt that way. "So what did you do about it?" he asked. I said, "Nothing." Then he gave me an assignment. He said he'd pray for my recovery, but I had to help.

"Every time you blow your nose, which may be pretty often, take a few seconds to ponder these words, 'Human opinion, individual or collective, cannot change God's will for me, which is health.'"

He was right. I blew my nose a lot that night, and pondered those words so often that I still remember them today.

On Thursday morning I could actually breathe through one nostril, and by noon both nostrils were clear and dry. I felt terrific, but since I had not studied for several days, I had lots of catching up to do.

After class on Thursday I realized there was no way to assimilate a week's worth of homework before the test, even if I crammed all night. I felt well, but not well enough to do the impossible, so I prayed for God's guidance and then listened. It occurred to me that the test was made of paper and ink, but this paper and ink claimed enough power to snatch me out of God's protection and send me into danger. I felt certain paper and ink could never be more powerful than God, and this certainty relaxed me, but I didn't fall asleep before remembering that my classmates were also guaranteed God's protection. Paper and ink couldn't harm them either.

On Friday morning, the atmosphere in the classroom was electric with tension. The exam was a 50-question multiple-choice test that would be quickly machine graded. We each had a sharp number 2 pencil when the starting bell sounded.

Usually on multiple-choice tests, one of the four answers to each question is absurd enough to rule out, leaving only three to choose from. I was shocked to find myself unable to identify even the absurd choice. It was clear I didn't have a prayer of passing the test, and whenever I don't have a prayer, I usually pray. I asked God silently but frankly, "What should I do? Maybe you know everything, but I don't." As I listened, a totally weird idea came to mind. As if spoken, it said, "You know how these tests look when complete. The little dots are spread unevenly all over the page. Since you don't know the answers, don't read the questions. Just 'draw' a completed test paper."

The idea seemed reckless, but what choice did I have? I was going to fail anyway. At least I could select one answer for each question. Maybe I'd get lucky on a few of them. Even a blind dog finds a bone sometimes.

After the tests were collected, it only took 15 minutes to grade them. Everyone except me could hardly wait to hear who would get his choice of duty stations after the course ended. The room was silent as the instructor returned, and after enjoying a dramatic moment, he revealed the results. "The highest grade in the class was earned by David Horn."

I tried not to look astonished, but I was in shock. This was totally impossible! Nobody is that lucky. He asked me which duty station I'd like to be sent to after the course ended, and I requested Washington, DC.

Never again did I earn the highest grade on a test, but we students all became best friends during our final two months at Bainbridge. Near the end of the course, we each received orders to our next duty station. I was ordered to the Naval Security Station on Nebraska Avenue in Washington DC, and the instructor had news for the rest of the class. He said it never happened before, but "not one sailor in this class received orders to a danger zone." He found that remarkable, and so did I.

In Navy jargon, my new job was at NAVSECSTA-WASHDC. Originally Mount Vernon Seminary for Girls, the Security Station was across Nebraska Avenue from the Swedish Embassy, and a few steps from American University. Guarded by Marines, nobody could enter without a top-secret clearance. Today it's part of the Department of Homeland Security.

The station stood on one of the highest points in Washington, DC. From our office windows, we could see the

Capitol dome, and the day after Martin Luther King, Jr. was assassinated, we saw smoke rising from burning buildings not far from the Capitol.

Work in the personnel department was interesting and routine. To keep us awake, a large percolator stayed warm all day until the coffee inside was strong enough to bend a spoon. One afternoon we staff were sitting around enjoying donuts when the chief asked each of us how we "ended up" in Washington.

One sailor said he came for R&R, rest and relaxation, after serving in Vietnam. Another had transferred to shore duty from an aircraft carrier. When my turn came, I explained that I earned the highest test score in my class at the training school and won the right to select a future duty station. I chose Washington.

That made the chief laugh. "The training school has no authority to guarantee anyone a choice of duty," he said. "They just said that to make you study harder. I distinctly recall the day the commander told me we needed another man from Bainbridge for our office. I opened the student files and picked you. That's the real reason you're here."

We all laughed, but I was confused, remembering how, as the result of prayer, I recovered from a severe head cold almost overnight, and how, as the result of prayer, I earned the highest grade on the test without reading the questions, and how none of my classmates were ordered into danger zones. Surely God was involved, and now this chief claimed credit for my being in Washington.

That evening after returning home, I sat down and asked God, "What really happened? Did you keep me safe by bringing me to Washington, or did the chief?"

I knew from experience how to recognize God's answer. It would be a thought I never thought before, and it would feel totally true. But until I stopped talking, I couldn't hear any answers, so I sat quietly and waited.

Before long, the answer came clear as a bell in these

words. "God does not partner with Uncle Sam to keep His children safe. God is a solo act. The divine Mind that guided your hand to the correct answers on the test also guided the chief's hand to select your name from the files. God does it all." Somehow, that had the ring of truth.

Chapel in the Pines—built by the SeeBees in 1963. I worshipped here during basic training at the Naval Construction Battalion Center in Davisville, Rhode Island.

🌿11

Return to Boston, again

*I*f all military personnel stationed in Washington DC during the Vietnam War had been uniformed, the Capitol would have looked like an occupied city. That's why enlisted personnel at the Naval Security Station wore winter blues or summer whites only at work. On nights and on weekends, we passed for civilians. With 90-minute lunch hours, one-dollar movies at the Bethesda Naval Hospital Theater and low-cost food at the Fort Myer Commissary, our life was good, until it got better.

On March 31, 1968, over 500,000 US troops were fighting in Vietnam when President Lyndon Johnson surprised us all by announcing on TV, "I shall not seek, nor will I accept, the nomination of my party for another term as your President." He wasn't just losing the war. He was running out of money to pay for it. To cut costs, some non-combatant enlisted personnel were offered a "six-month early out." My two-year enlistment suddenly became 18 months, so I declined a generous reenlistment bonus and prepared to resume civilian life in Boston. I'd seen clear evidence of God's fingerprints while on active duty, and Providence wasn't done with me yet.

Before checking job openings in the CSPS Personnel Department, I walked into Monitor Advertising and surprised old friends. They were having a difficult day. One of the correspondents who supported the Monitor Advertising Representatives had just learned a baby she hoped to adopt from Europe would arrive the next morning. She was resigning when I appeared at the door with exactly the qualifications needed for her job. After a short interview, her position was offered and I accepted. The manager, Zadie Hatfield, told me, "Go down to Personnel and tell them we've already hired you. It was providential that you came now."

In those days the Monitor printed five regional editions daily, each with local ads. Who sold these ads? In any city or town with a Christian Science church, one member would volunteer to be an "Ad Rep," visiting local merchants regularly to offer advertising space in the Monitor. Some larger firms bought display ads, especially at Christmas, but "Mom and Pop" stores usually purchased business cards appearing in columns on the back page of each edition under "City Headings."

The question Ad Reps heard most was, "Why should I advertise my shoe repair shop in an international newspaper? Wouldn't my advertising dollar be better spent at our local paper?"

We had a unique answer to that question—proof of purchase (POP) receipts. Christian Science church members received booklets of blank POP receipts. After shopping at a Monitor advertiser, a member would tell the storeowner an ad in the Monitor had caught his or her eye, and later fill out a POP receipt including date of purchase and how much was spent. Members dropped completed receipts into collection boxes in the lobbies of Christian Science churches from coast to coast. Before revisiting a customer to ask for more advertising, the Monitor Ad Rep would empty the box, arrange the receipts by store, and give them to the business owner as token proof that Monitor advertising improved his business.

My responsibility as correspondent was to inspire volunteer Ad Reps to visit more retailers and sell more ads. I reminded them of Mary Baker Eddy's mission for her newspaper, "to injure no man, but to bless all mankind," assuring them that Monitor advertising enabled local merchants to support this noble mission and would inevitably improve their bottom line, since blessings always boomerang.

Most Ad Reps believed blessings sometimes boomerang, but not always. One Rep told me she flatly refused to revisit a gasoline station and ask for more ads since she never received a single POP receipt proving anyone purchased fuel there. It would be dishonest to solicit an ad without any proof of purchase, she said. So you can imagine how surprised she was when the station owner phoned her wishing to buy more ads. Her honesty kicked in, and she asked bluntly, "Why on earth would you do that? The Monitor isn't a charity, and I've never seen any proof that our members patronize your business."

"That may be true," he said, "but I can't tell you how often drivers from distant cities pull off the Interstate at my exit to fill up. They say they read the Monitor at home and noticed my ad before leaving on their trip. I want to keep attracting them." Who knows? Maybe some blessings boomerang in ways we can't measure?

While nurturing Monitor Ad Reps, I obtained two new, tailored business suits at no cost, for ushering in The Mother Church.

In those days, male ushers wore identical tan suits in summer and black suits in winter. New ushers received coupons to visit Read & White Formal Wear on Summer Street in downtown Boston, where we were fitted for both suits. We could wear them anywhere, anytime, and keep them when we left the usher staff.

Besides receiving new suits, ushers became privy to the inner workings of The Mother Church. The sound system, for example, included a small brown box concealed in the hymnal rack of each pew. This box contained a microphone and speaker. During Wednesday evening testimony meetings, members and visitors would speak from the floor about healings they had through prayer, and their remarks were amplified in a unique way.

Downstairs near the foyer, an unmarked door concealed what was known during WWII as the Radio Room. From

here during the war a transmitter broadcast live church services to Europe, including Nazi Germany. When I was ushering, the room served a different purpose. Each Wednesday
evening when someone rose to speak from the floor, an engineer in the Radio Room used a device similar to radar to
"sweep" the auditorium. As soon as a blip of light located the
speaker's voice, he turned up the nearest microphone and
turned down all others. The testifier's voice was then reproduced, but not amplified, through every other hymnal rack
speaker. This process took about 10 seconds, and a few visitors believed their hearing had improved when an indistinct
distant voice suddenly became crystal clear. If the testifier
spoke too softly to be identified by the "radar" downstairs,
the engineer would press a button illuminating a small light
on the Reader's desk, prompting him to ask, "Would you
speak a little louder, please?"

But First Readers had more to do than watch for a light.
They also had to watch the clock. To allow as many as possible to speak, remarks were limited to three minutes. If a
speaker rambled and time grew short, the Reader might in-
terrupt, "Are you coming to the healing part soon?" But one
Wednesday the Reader's reminder brought down the house
with laughter.

A testifier explained that he'd been diagnosed by a doctor with a fatal disease and given one year to live. He called
a Christian Science practitioner for prayerful help, but became scared after six months and returned to the doctor for
another check-up. Now he was told he had six months to
live. Desperate, he returned to the practitioner and prayed
daily. After three months, he visited the doctor again to see
if he was better, and was given a fearful verdict—only three
months left to live. Determined to trust God for his healing,
he continued in prayer, and soon felt much better, so he returned to the doctor to confirm his healing and was warned
he might die within a month.

In hindsight, we assume the First Reader found this testimony monotonous and let his mind wander as he watched the second hand on his clock. Just before three minutes elapsed, he looked up and said firmly, "Sir, you have one-half minute left!" Nobody in the congregation could stop laughing.

Some say laughter is the best medicine, but my experience since boyhood suggested prayer might also be a healing agent so, while working in Monitor advertising, I applied for what Christian Scientists call "class instruction" or "Primary Class." Church employees received full salary during the two-week course.

Over the years, my parents and I often called a Christian Science practitioner for prayerful help solving problems. I thought maybe someday I'd like to be a practitioner, and class instruction was the first requirement. Classes are taught by practitioners whose healing ability qualifies them for additional training called Normal Class. After taking Normal Class, practitioners become teachers and may offer class instruction.

My mother's teacher was Lavinia Butterworth (Mrs. B) in Philadelphia, but she had passed away so I interviewed several teachers in the Boston area. All were welcoming and kind, but only one really clicked because he was so fatherly. His name was Charles Henry Gabriel, Clerk of The Mother Church. He'd been teaching two years, and accepted me into his third annual class.

I didn't know what to expect the first day. There were 30 men and women in the class, and we all sat on folding chairs in the former boardroom of The Mother Church extension. Mr. Gabriel's desk was at one end on a slightly raised platform, next to a spinet piano. Above the fireplace, a portrait of Mary Baker Eddy smiled down on us.

Our first day (and each following day for two weeks) was opened by singing hymn 151, which begins, "In speechless prayer and reverence, Dear Lord, I come to thee."

Afterward, using the chapter "Recapitulation" from the

Christian Science textbook as an outline, Mr. Gabriel explained how healing is achieved through prevailing prayer. Sometimes he'd clarify a point with a personal experience.

One Sunday morning, for example, he was called by parents staying on the second floor of the Midtown Motor Inn, across from The Mother Church. Their young son had wandered out of the room and accidentally slipped through the railing, falling onto the concrete pool deck one floor below. His head was cut and bleeding, so he ran back to the room, wrapped a towel around his head and wriggled under a bed. He was scared and refused to come out. Could Mr. Gabriel pray for him?

Our teacher agreed to pray, but also offered to drive to the motel immediately to see the lad.

He admitted being concerned for the boy's safety, and prayed for reassurance from God. It came sooner than he expected. Just before arriving at the motel, he saw a movie marquee announcing in bold letters, BORN FREE. This reminded him that every child of God is born free of fear or danger, and this restored his faith.

When he arrived, both parents were distressed because the boy refused to come out from under the bed. It was almost time for church, so he asked them to go across the street to The Mother Church. "Don't try to apply everything you hear to your son," he urged them. "Just enjoy the service." Eventually they left, and the room was silent.

That's when Mr. Gabriel removed his coat, vest and tie. He stretched out on the carpet and crawled under the bed where the young boy was very surprised to see him. He introduced himself and after they chatted a moment, he asked, "Would we be more comfortable sitting in a chair?" The boy agreed, so they both crawled out from beneath the bed. The boy sat on his lap in a chair, but refused to unwrap the bloody towel. "Well," asked Mr. Gabriel, "how about if we just unwrap one inch of it?" That was okay. Then a few more inches, until before long, the towel was soaking in the sink.

Mr. Gabriel told us, "He and I sang the hymn 'Shepherd show me how to go,' and as I looked down, I could see the cut on his head closing before my eyes. There was no fear in the room, and after a few minutes, he looked up at me and said, 'I think you're the best friend I have in Boston.'"

When the parents returned from church, their son was happy and well, and the towel was drying on the shower rod.

Several weeks later, Mr. Gabriel was walking down Massachusetts Avenue near The Mother Church when this couple and their son approached. The boy recognized him and ran ahead to give him a hug. "Oh Mr. Gabriel," he said, "do you remember that swell healing WE had?" It was true. They both were healed of fear that day.

And what was the point of the story? As we listened closely, our teacher made it clear. Always be willing to meet a patient wherever he seems to be, but never forget where he really is —safe in the presence of God.

After two weeks of continuous inspiration, as we prepared to adjourn, Mr. Gabriel gave us a farewell wish. "May it always be said of my pupils that they are sweet." It was a wish we carried with us for the rest of our lives.

After two happy years in Monitor advertising, I transferred to what most newspapers call the morgue. We called it the reference library, where reporters research their news stories and editorials. In addition to many shelves of reference books, we had about five million news clippings in six tall Lektriever filing machines, arranged alphabetically by subject. Newspapers didn't have online archives yet, so reporters would call and ask for clippings on Israeli agriculture or Ronald Reagan or Ford Motor Company. We had no master file of subjects. It was all in our heads. The longer you worked in the library, the more subjects you knew and the more valuable you were.

Often reporters would rush in with a question. When this happened, we followed two unbreakable rules. First, get the correct answer. Second, get it in 15 minutes. After a few years under this regimen, I began doing everything in 15-minute intervals. I'd mow the lawn, wash the car, or take a bath, always in 15 minutes.

One of the questions reporters asked most often was how to spell the names of Palestinian refugee camps. If a foreign correspondent wasn't sure, he passed the buck to the copy desk by spelling them two ways in the same story. Most names had multiple English spellings, but could we find the correct spelling in 15 minutes?

The Palestinian Liberation Organization (PLO) had no embassy in Washington DC, but they did have a mission at the United Nations in New York City. I called them with questions like this, and a lady named Rhonda always answered the phone sweetly. "Good morning! PLO. Can I help you?" The PLO was a terrorist organization, so I listened for gunshots or at least a grunt in the background, but heard only Rhonda. She was charming and could spell all the camp names perfectly. She helped us as much as possible, hoping the Monitor might print a kind word about the PLO. Sometimes we did, but not often.

The reference library was adjacent to the newsroom, and whenever "big wigs" came to address the newsroom staff, we stood along the wall and listened. That's how I met 1984 presidential candidate Jesse Jackson, and United Nations Secretary General Kurt Waldheim. When Waldheim shook my hand, he behaved as if I was more important than he was. I've never forgotten that unusual feeling.

🌿*12*

Never lonely again

*D*espite frequent evidence of God's fingerprints on my life, Providence was not a good matchmaker. By my 34th birthday, I had no children and two failed marriages under my belt. I longed to be a dad, but time was running out, so I practiced for parenthood as a pretend uncle.

A golden "uncle-tunity" came after I gave a travelogue slide show, "From Maine to Florida," to patients at the Tenacre Foundation in Princeton, New Jersey. Tenacre is a care facility for Christian Scientists seeking healing through prayer, and has a beautiful circular dining room with large windows overlooking the woods. One evening at supper I met a staff member named Rose, a single mom with two little children. They lived in a modest, two bedroom apartment in nearby Lawrenceville. We gradually became close friends and she invited me to spend the weekend in a motel near her apartment. After splashing in the apartment swimming pool, we enjoyed supper together around her kitchen table, and once the kids were tucked in, Rose and I talked until midnight, mostly about Christian Science. Our friendship was platonic, and I visited several weekends that year. We both needed a friend, and I needed to uncle.

After each return to Boston, I recorded exciting bedtime stories (with sound effects) on cassette tapes and mailed them to Rose for her children. I also sent funny cards and holiday gifts. During one of my visits, as we played a children's game on the floor, Rose's daughter Yvonne suddenly stopped, took both my hands in hers, looked up at me and said, "I love you." It was a complete surprise, so I said I loved her too, never dreaming she really meant it. Over time our

lives moved gently apart, and we lost touch for the next thir-
ty-two years.

In 2012 I was guest speaker at a church workshop in
Charlotte, North Carolina. Members from several states attended, and during lunch a lady approached to say my talk
inspired her and she was grateful. "You don't remember me,
do you?" she asked, and I surely didn't.

"My name is Yvonne."

Then it all came back. This was the little girl who loved
me. I never expected to see her again. Now she was training
to be a Christian Science nurse, a career demanding almost
endless love. She thanked me for "fathering" her briefly when
she was young. She remembered everything—the recorded
bedtime stories, the gifts and the cards. She believed my fatherly affection helped her to understand love and succeed
in life. Before that day, I never knew a pretend uncle could
accomplish so much good. Imagine what a real father could
do! But fatherhood was nowhere in sight.

Meanwhile, back in Boston, a little boy named Peter
needed an uncle. When he was in elementary school, he'd
sit on my lap strumming his plastic ukulele and we'd sing,
"The people on the bus go up and down, up and down, up
and down," again and again. We enjoyed lunching at Mc-
Donald's, and once, on the way to see his namesake movie,
"Pete's Dragon," he pointed out that if I married his mom,
he and I could spend every day together. But that was not
to be.

Pete loved camping, so when I told his mom about the
Lake Pemaquid Campground in Damariscotta, Maine, she
offered to drive if I'd point the way. We had enough time to
stay overnight, so she brought a tent for her, Peter and his
sister Lori, and I packed a pup tent for myself.

While she and her kids organized their site, I was free
to stroll the campground's leafy lanes. Bachelorhood seldom
felt lonely in Boston, where singles were everywhere, but at a
family campground all I saw were parents with playful chil-

dren and a dog or two. It was depressing, so I asked God for any idea to help relieve my isolation. And then, as usual, I listened expectantly.

Before long, a verse from the Bible came to mind. "And I, if I be lifted up from the earth, will draw all men unto me." (John 12: 32 KJV) As a child in Sunday school, I learned that Jesus was urging his followers to lift up, or pay attention to his spiritual nature, the Christ. But in her writings, Mary Baker Eddy includes several definitions of the Christ. Which one should I lift up in my thought?

After listening a little longer, I remembered she once defined Christ as the spiritual idea of sonship. And what is that? Obviously it's the idea that we all have the same Father, God, and in His eyes we're all one family, with no one left out. I pondered this idea and it comforted me. All these parents and kids were actually my relatives, because God was our common Father. But was this really true? After reading what happened next, you decide.

Free of loneliness, with a new spring in my step, I came to a small play area with five children on swings. I watched quietly until one child and called, "Please give us a push!" Thanks to big pushes, each one was soon swinging skyward, and after being pushed, each child said, "Thank you." I called them "the please and thank-you gang," and we very naturally learned each other's names. They were from two families who camped at Lake Pemaquid each summer for two weeks. They said they always returned to the playground before bed to tell ghost stories. I offered to join them that night and tell a story they'd never forget. Then we all hurried back to our campsites for supper over open fires.

Just as the sun was setting, we reunited at the playground, and their parents came too. The children told them at supper about a single man who offered to meet them after dark, and this may have raised a red flag. But it came down quickly when I explained that I worked for the Christian

Science Monitor. All four parents were schoolteachers who used the Monitor in their classrooms. They held it in high esteem, and were glad to trust their children to an employee of the much respected newspaper.

Beneath an ebony blanket of stars, I told them the story of "Lost Horizon," from the 1937 movie starring Ronald Colman. My new friends hung on every word about the Utopian lost world of Shangri-La, hidden deep in the Himalayan Mountains, a paradise where all are happy and content because no one in the outside world believes Shangri-La exists, so no one disturbs its bliss. Before we parted, I asked them, "Do you believe in Shangri-La?" They didn't, but wished they could.

In my pup tent that night, I decided to buy these children a modest gift, and the next morning gave each one a souvenir comb from the camp store.

Their parents told me the kids were excited when they returned to their tents for the night, and decided to pool their allowance to buy me a farewell gift, a small figurine of the Ancient Mariner. Before I left for Boston, we all took pictures of each other and hugged goodbye. By accepting God as everyone's father, I'd found wonderful new friends.

Then something went very wrong. Back in the city, I began planning to see these kids again. Maybe we could be pen pals during the winter and meet again next summer at Lake Pemaquid. I phoned the campground office and asked for help. Could they identify campers if I provided first names? They were sorry, but they could not help. Since I didn't know their last names, these dear children were gone forever. I again felt the pain of two divorces, where reconciliation was impossible and all my hopes and dreams went up in smoke. Now these children were gone too. I knew I didn't deserve disappointment, and I was angry with God. If He really was love, then He knew He owed me an explanation, so I sat on the sofa in my living room and almost shouted, "Why do you keep doing this to me? Must I be lonely all my life?" I refused to move until He answered my question.

He must have known I was serious, because after I waited half-an-hour expectantly, an idea came that changed my life forever.

"You thought you saw five faces on the playground. In truth, you only saw one face. It was my face. From now on, wherever you are, always look for my face, and you will never be lonely again."

Instinctively I knew this was absolutely true, and hurried outside to look for God's face—evidence of His universal love—in everyone I met. I saw God's face in the accuracy and efficiency of the cashier at the food market, and in the precise care my barber showed when cutting my hair, and in the extreme accuracy of reporters on the Monitor newsroom staff. I was so busy looking for God's face that I forgot to feel lonely.

A few months later, I shared this experience during a Wednesday evening testimony meeting at a Christian Science church near Boston. It resonated with a young single mom in the congregation. Her name was Evelyn. She saw God's face in me, and I saw God's face in her. She had two little girls. They weren't twins, but they each had God's face. We married in 1982, and ever since then we've enjoyed looking for God's face together. As you will see, it's been a spiritual adventure.

Evelyn and I on our wedding day, August 14, 1982. During the ceremony, the minister prayed, "May each one who is touched by the union of Evelyn and David feel part of your impartial plan of universal blessing. May Michelle and Nicole gain from this marriage a clear sense of your ever-present Father-Motherhood. In Jesus' name we ask it. Amen."

13

What is a househusband?

*I*n his 1938 play, "Our Town," Thornton Wilder tells the story of everyday life in the fictional American town of Grover's Corners from 1901 to 1913. A hit on Broadway, "Our Town" won a Pulitzer Prize for Drama and is still staged today.

In the play, childhood neighbors George and Emily marry after high school and start a family. Nine years later, Emily dies giving birth to their second child. After her funeral, Emily emerges to join the dead seated quietly in the cemetery. They encourage her to forget her life, but she insists on returning to earth to relive one day, her 12th birthday. The memories prove too painful, and she realizes that every moment of life should be treasured. Near the end of the play, she asks the Stage Manager if anyone truly understands the value of life while they live it. "No," he replies. "The saints and poets, maybe—they do some."

When Evelyn and I married in 1982, I was neither a saint nor a poet, but appreciated life by then and had the advantage of starting family life later than usual. Her two daughters didn't know it yet, but they would spend the next decade patiently teaching me to be a dad.

As soon as Evelyn and I returned from our honeymoon in Rockport, Massachusetts, I gathered the girls and explained that everyone on earth gets one dad. Since they already had one, they should call me Dave. Even without the official title, I couldn't wait to enjoy the laughter and tears of fatherhood, and when Nicole started first grade and Michelle began third, I felt keenly these lyrics of a song from the early 20th century musical "Babes in Toyland," by Victor

Herbert. "Toyland, Toyland, dear little girl and boy land. While you dwell within it, you are ever happy then. Childhood joy-land, mystical merry Toyland. Once you pass its borders you can ne'er return again."

I began by capturing our life together on film, creating album after album of family photos with descriptive captions, all in date order. Like windows to a forgotten yesterday, these snapshots show us visiting Mary Baker Eddy's historic home in Chestnut Hill, swimming in Walden Pond, touring Louisa May Alcott's home in Concord, sitting in Mary's seat at the restored one-room school house in Sudbury where Mary had a little lamb, and meeting Mickey at Disney World.

After a few months, we had developed family rituals. Each Saturday morning I'd walk to Dunkin' Donuts with a list of eight choices—two donuts for each of us. We split a cheese pizza at Papa Gino's every Saturday night before tuning the radio to "A Prairie Home Companion." I almost lost my voice yelling "Go, Blue Bullets!!!" at Nicole's soccer games, and helped Michelle create a replica of Buckingham Palace using only scissors, a cardboard box and gray spray paint. It wasn't an exact replica, but it earned a B.

After ten years in the Monitor reference library, I was ready for something new and Evelyn missed the workaday world. She had become a stay-at-home mom after our wedding, but longed to punch the time clock again, so we swapped places. She returned to an office, and I became a househusband.

What exactly is a househusband? I had only a vague idea when she rejoined her carpool. "This is a piece of cake," I thought, sleeping late the first morning, and I was partly right. Househusbanding can be a cinch if you appreciate a well-vacuumed rug and know what goes with what, clothes-wise, on little girls. Gourmet cooking is optional since most children prefer Kraft macaroni and hot dogs. It sounds pretty trivial, and it can be unless you look deeper. Some people have a knack for making homes out of houses. They can convert an empty-all-day split ranch into a living, breathing activity center, and some of these people are men.

I took over during the summer, which is trial-by-fire time in the suburbs. School is closed, and children all over town are falling victim to their eternal enemy, boredom. I quickly learned where all the free beaches were, and when the ice cream truck jingled down our street, my wallet was open. The local library offered endless air-conditioned entertainment, and now and then we'd go to a fast food outlet ("the one with the playground, please!") We washed the car and each other with the garden hose, and grilled burgers outside night after night after night.

Sure I missed the office, the whirr of copiers, the endless phone calls, and especially the paycheck. But summer was a time to be lazy, a vital rest period for growing children and me.

When school started that fall, Michelle and I argued a few times each week about whether her hair was wet or damp, since I would not let her leave for school with wet hair. And I became "room dad" for Nicole's third grade class, calling the mothers to see who could bake what for parties. On rainy afternoons, I edged our yellow Ford Pinto close to the school's front door. With the back seat folded flat, I could squeeze six or eight poncho-wrapped third graders under the hatch, packed together like sardines. Moms might not do this, but my crew was giggly and dry.

I earned a modest income by writing business biographies for a publisher and doing ad-layout two nights a week at the Metro-West News, while Michelle and Nicole remained the lights of my life. They made all my dreams come true.

But how could I be certain the girls really accepted me as part of their family? They were happy and obedient, and we all seemed close, but for more than a year the Ghost of Divorces Past stood by my chair whispering "this too shall end."

Without knowing it, Michelle helped me banish that ghost forever, in a very unexpected way.

One night when she was in fifth grade she went to bed with an upset stomach. A few hours later, as we all slept soundly, she suddenly woke and threw up. She felt much better afterward, but needed help to remove the soiled sheets and put on clean ones. It was a messy job to do quietly in semi-darkness, so she tiptoed into the bedroom where Evelyn and I were sleeping and wakened me instead of her mom.

I knew that, under such circumstances, nobody would wake someone they didn't love and trust. It was almost an honor to clean up her bed, and tuck her in between fresh clean sheets. I gave her a quick kiss goodnight, and never again heard the fearful warning, "this too shall end." It never ended. We're still buddies today.

When I was growing up, the term "mother-in-law" was often pejorative. A few newlyweds called these supplemental parents Mom, but usually mothers-in-law received dual monikers like Mother Benson or Mother Smith, and with the best intentions, they sometimes behaved like "Mother Superior."

So imagine my surprise when Evelyn introduced me to her mom—a woman so devoid of criticism, so unwilling to take sides, so invisible even when visiting overnight, that I describe her to friends as "the mother-in-law from heaven."

Her name was Betty, and she knew the way to a man's heart is through his stomach. She was living with Evelyn when we met, and babysat the girls during our first date at Longfellow's Wayside Inn. Betty discovered my favorite foods, and whenever I visited Evelyn she had several quarts of homemade potato salad and at least two dozen deviled eggs in the fridge. She said they were "too much" and insisted I take some home.

Betty had survived the Great Depression and knew the value of a dollar. She wore the same comfortable winter coat until it was threadbare, and when she received a red plastic children's wristwatch as a prize at Burger King, she wore it every day until the battery died.

Until I met Betty, I never knew anyone who washed and reused cellophane. When Michelle and Nicole were little and had sniffles, Betty cut all the tissue boxes in the house in half, so they'd last twice as long.

Like many of her generation, Betty saved string. Cleaning out her attic one day, I found a brown paper bag containing several balls of old string, and also a small box filled with tiny bits of twine. The box was clearly marked, "String too short to save."

Betty may have been a packrat, but she was never a tightwad. At 80, she refused to re-carpet her living room because, "I'll never live long enough to enjoy it." But she spent freely on airline tickets and her travels made Secretary of State John Kerry look like a homebody. In addition to visiting nearly all fifty states, she had toured England, Europe, Morocco (where she rode a camel), Japan, Hong Kong and China.

Can you guess what souvenirs she brought home to remember these journeys? Candid snapshots and matchbooks, because matchbooks were always free, even in China. On all her many travels, she never met a stranger. She could sit on a park bench and chat easily with whoever sat beside her.

Betty liked to work as much as play. When she was 50 and secretarial jobs became scarce, she returned to college to earn her bachelor's and master's degrees and a little toward a Ph.D. All these diplomas guaranteed her a job teaching first grade far beyond retirement age at a nearby elementary school.

But for me, Betty's finest role was as a mother-in-law. In all the years I knew her, I never once heard her complain. Even at 92, when told she might live one more year, she simply said, "that's okay." She was not a martyr, but she had no time for self-pity.

Betty's joy came from the little things in life, and her

favorite collectibles were colorful paper placemats used in rural restaurants. She admired placemats showing birds or barns or sunken treasures, and often asked the waitress for a fresh one to take home, where she'd tape it to her kitchen wall.

Betty is gone now, but it's no secret where she went. Recently Evelyn and I remembered her when we visited a pancake house and noticed placemats with pictures of covered bridges.

"I hope they have placemats in heaven," Evelyn said softly. "Amen," I replied.

When Governor Mike Dukakis ran for President in 1988, he boasted about what he called the Massachusetts Miracle. For many of us living in the Bay State, it felt like a miracle. Between 1982, when Evelyn and I were married, and 1988, state unemployment fell from 11 per cent to less than 4 per cent. State budgets were balanced, deficits were eliminated and taxes were cut. As people earned more, they looked for larger homes, causing a spike in real estate prices. Inflation was creeping upward, and when Federal Reserve Chairman Paul Volcker tried to choke it by raising the prime interest rate to a whooping 21.5 per cent in 1981, the message was clear. "Buy your house now, before rates go higher." By 1984, Massachusetts' real estate was so hot that home hunters often carried a deposit in their pocket.

Evelyn and I rode the crest of this wave, buying a three-bedroom, one-bath ranch in Framingham in 1984 for $80,000. When we first toured the empty home, three other potential buyers and their realtors were parked out front, waiting, so we put down our deposit on the spot, and it was a good investment. As the girls advanced through elementary school, our home appreciated $15,000 every 12 months.

But bubbles have a way of bursting, and the Massachusetts Miracle was approaching a climax. Beside that, Betty was living alone in rural Indiana and could use some family support, even though she'd never ask for it. So we sold our house at the height of the Miracle for $140,000. The new owners felt it was such a bargain that they brought champagne to the closing.

We had no jobs waiting, but with surplus from the sale of our home we moved anyway. For the next twenty years, we'd be Hoosiers, and Indiana would be very good to us.

14

Back home again in Indiana

*B*etty still lived in the lakeside cottage in rural Bremen, where Evelyn spent girlhood summers and attended her senior year of high school. We all crowded in with her for a few months until we found a home in nearby Plymouth, the Marshall County seat. The Massachusetts Miracle had not inflated home prices in Indiana, and the historic three-bedroom, two-bath home we selected near town was owned by the county attorney. He was holding out for $40,000, "not a penny less," so we paid cash.

Betty had warned us, "There are no jobs out here," and she was right. For several months we lived on savings and my modest income as a substitute teacher.

In Indiana at that time, substitute teachers did not need physical exams or a background check. Anyone who could produce a college diploma and a $5 bill at the same time could buy a substitute teaching license with certification to teach anything from first grade to middle school woodshop to third year French.

Anyone who ever subbed knows it's like making a cold sales call. You don't know where you're working until the morning you arrive, and the students don't know who to expect until you get there. I registered for "elementary grades only" in five adjoining rural school districts and got called several days a week. Routines at each school were similar. Take attendance, collect lunch money and select a child to carry it to the office, pledge allegiance to the flag—students expected this, but wondered what the substitute might do next. In order to know the class better without being intrusive, I passed out blank sheets of lined paper and asked everyone to "write down something about yourself that no-body else knows. Don't sign your name! Then pass them forward and I'll read them aloud and we'll see if anyone can guess which secret is yours." These kids had been friends for years, and had never been asked to do this before, so they were curious. They learned more about each other than they knew before, and so did I.

On Monday morning, spelling words for the week were announced, along with their definitions. A real teacher does this very seriously, reading each new word clearly and then using it in a sentence. As a sub, I felt free to read each word and then use it in a funny sentence with a British accent. Students were always surprised and could not help laughing.

If the teacher left a lesson plan, I tried to follow it, interrupted mercifully by morning recess, lunch, 30 minutes out of class for art or gym, and afternoon recess followed by water fountain and bathroom visits, and maybe a game of hangman on the blackboard until the busses arrived.

Some days were better than others, but my best was a fourth grade class at Washington Elementary in Plymouth. The teacher let me observe on Monday and Tuesday (without pay) until I took her place on Wednesday, Thursday and Friday. She had something called "centers," parts of the room where kids did different assignments, rotating from one center to another every 15 minutes for an hour. She hosted the reading center, where each child read to her. Each boy and girl was very familiar with the drill and knew exactly where he or she should be at any given moment. With their help, each day ran smoothly and they were very proud of me for learning their system. I got some pats on the back, and on Friday afternoon they wanted to gather around me for a group photo. The snapshot was smudged, but I didn't mind. It was You Know Who's fingerprint.

Plymouth was also home to the Pilot-News, the only daily newspaper in Marshall County. After years in the hands of a respected local family, it was sold to a company which owned many other newspapers and several radio stations. Budgets were slashed so severely that, when the newsroom converted from typewriters to computers, the new owners refused to pay extra for a feature called "spell-check," since reporters had survived without it until then. Each slim daily paper would have as many as 20 typos, which I began circling in red as I caught up on the news. Finally, with time on my hands, I visited the newsroom and volunteered to proof read each story for free. The editor was so impressed that he hired me on the spot as a new reporter and asked me to begin work the next week.

The newsroom staff was surprised when I showed up on time. "We didn't expect you," they said frankly. "Why would someone who worked at the Christian Science Monitor want to work here?" I told them it was because of my kids. They were addicted to food and had to eat three times a day, and I had to support their habit. That explanation made sense to everyone, since we all earned "peanuts."

Some believe small newspapers are plum assignments for journalists, and this is partly true. Day after day includes the usual drudgery—a walk to the sheriff's office for the police report; telephone calls to all three funeral homes to copy down obituaries; and monthly evening assignments covering school board and town board meetings which can last until midnight, drenched in monotony or acrimony.

The most tedious school board meeting I ever covered was in a small town south of Plymouth. The agenda seemed endless, and sometime after 11 p.m. one of the school busses was discussed. Its engine had been misfiring and the driver felt it needed new sparkplugs. He delivered one of the plugs to the superintendent, who presented it at the meeting where it was passed around the board table, each member giving an opinion whether it needed replacement or not. I sank bone-tired in my corner chair and wondered, "Does it get any worse than this?"

My goal was to bring Monitor-quality journalism to the

Pilot-News, and even in what appeared to be tiresome meetings, there were opportunities to do this.

One night I was covering the town board meeting in Argos, Indiana. The agenda was long, as usual, and I was trying to capture key comments and final decisions for the next day's paper.

Halfway through the meeting, the town marshal stood up and asked the board for $200 so the Just Say No Club at the junior high could hire a popular disc jockey from South Bend to host a school dance designed to keep kids away from drugs. The board chair explained there was no line item in the budget for this expense, so "come back next year." It only took three minutes of a three-hour meeting, but it was my lead. I reported every detail of the meeting accurately, and led with the headline, "Board Refuses Funds to Just Say No Club Students." Can you guess the result?

The town marshal called me the next evening and said that after the Pilot-News hit the streets at 3 p.m., "My phone started ringing off the hook. I accepted donations from local residents until we had $200, and after that I only took pledges, in case there was a future need. By bedtime, do you know how much money was pledged? If we wanted to, we could send the entire Just Say No Club on a trip to Hawaii." That was the first time I realized the power of even a small newspaper. Most people will do the right thing if they're sure what it is.

In our six-person newsroom, a police scanner always crackled softly in the background, usually broadcasting routine traffic, but if we heard the siren from the volunteer fire department down the street, we turned up the scanner for details. Often the dispatcher at the police station next door would announce a 1050PI.

"Ten Codes" are signals used since 1940 by law enforcement in two-way radio communication as numeric code words for frequent messages. The numbers 1050 mean "accident" and the letters PI mean "personal injury." When we heard the location on the scanner, one of the reporters would grab a camera and note pad and drive to the site, often following a fire engine.

One day the siren started wailing and we listened for a Ten Code, but heard nothing. Finally the dispatcher said something we'd never heard before. "Plane in distress over the airport." Now that was news! Everyone grabbed a camera and we all drove to the airport to learn more details.

In those days, Plymouth Airport was a long grass strip, with a terminal building about the size of a Wendy's. It was used almost entirely by private planes, and none were ever in distress. As we approached the field, we noticed something very unusual. The usually competitive city police, county police and state police were all cooperating. Several fire engines were present, along with a few ambulances. A Piper Cub was circling high above the field. What could be wrong?

A few miles south of Plymouth on the shore of Lake Maxinkuckee is the tiny town of Culver. Its claim to fame is the famous Culver Military Academy, a co-ed private school founded in 1894. In the early 1990's, the academy included a Naval School with a three-masted schooner sailing on the lake, and an Aviation School where cadets in high school could prepare to earn a pilot's license. Notable alumni include actor Hal Holbrook, George Steinbrenner, principal owner of the New York Yankees, and 1940 GOP presidential nominee Wendell Willkie.

This had been a routine day at the academy airfield, with training planes taking off and landing regularly, but one takeoff was not routine. A student pilot was at the controls, and as the plane gained altitude the control tower radioed that one of the two front landing wheels had fallen off. The pilot circled low for visual inspection and the observation was confirmed. One wheel was missing. The instructor took over the controls and radioed Plymouth airport, since it had a longer grass runway. He would need to land there.

Local motorists passing the airport saw a sea of flashing

red lights and many pulled over until the berm was filled with cars and trucks. One lady told me, "I didn't know what the problem was, so I just sat, parked and prayed."

Conversation between the Plymouth control tower and the circling plane was patched to the public address system as we reporters took positions along the edge of the field, cameras ready. I was at the far end, where the plane would either stop or burst into flames. A row of two fire trucks and two ambulances were lined up to drive side-by-side behind the plane as it landed. Finally we all heard the pilot say, "Okay, after one more circle, I'm bringing it down."

All eyes were glued on the training plane as it crossed low over the parked cars on the roadway and just above the row of emergency vehicles. As the vehicles moved forward protectively behind it, the instructor tipped the wings at an angle and landed on one wheel. He balanced the plane on that wheel all the way down the runway, slower and slower, until finally it stopped and gently dropped its raised wing to the grass. The plane was not damaged and nobody was hurt.

When the young, uniformed cadet stepped out of the plane, I asked him if he'd been afraid during the landing. "Oh, no sir!" he said sincerely. "I have complete faith in my instructor." We all were grateful to report a happy ending to what could have been a tragedy.

Our editor urged reporters to scour the county for feature stories. He claimed "news never happens in the newsroom," but sometimes it does. One of the town's best known characters was a grizzled old retired farmer who loved to sit and chat with anyone. Often he came in the newsroom to while away some time. His visits usually interrupted our work, but one morning he settled beside my desk and said, "Did I ever tell you about the time I pushed over a privy?" I smelled a possible feature story and asked him to continue.

He said it happened when he was just a lad. The family living on the farm across the road had a "two-holer"—an outhouse with a large hole for adults and a smaller one for children. One day, for no apparent reason, their four-year-old daughter tried to sit on the adult hole and fell through. Her terrified mother knew what happened and was helpless to save the child, so she ran across the road and found a teen-age boy (now the old man sitting beside me) and begged him to help. I recall his exact words.

"There was no way I could fit through the adult hole, so I had to shove the privy over on its side. Then I jumped into the hole and fished the girl out. I handed her up to her mother, who rushed her inside and scrubbed her clean. But I had to sleep in the barn for the next two weeks!"

I used this fragrant recollection to open a story about the history of outhouses, debunking the myth that they were invented by Thomas Crapper (England, 1836-1910). He held several patents for plumbing products, but not the water closet.

The Pilot-News always needed feature photos to fill holes on news pages. Often I'd leave after deadline and drive around the county with a camera searching for unique pictures. Reader favorites were candid shots of students in school. Parents would buy multiple copies of the paper to send these photos to relatives, and one always ended up in the family album. As a former substitute teacher, I was a familiar face at school offices and had carte blanche to roam the halls and enter any room at random to snap photos. Teachers welcomed me, because everyone knew I only took pictures of kids hard at work. So when I entered a room, everyone got busy.

The best school photos were taken in biology lab the day children dissected frogs. Facial expressions were price-less. Photos of children painting pictures in art class were also popular, as well as snapshots of a high school swimming class taken from the underwater pool window. But the best photo I ever took never got in the paper. It was never even developed.

One day I was visiting various rooms at the new Bourbon Elementary School. One young lady really wanted her photo taken, so she was extremely serious and busy at her desk. Her eyes followed me as I strolled around the room taking photos, and then I realized I was out of film, so I quietly walked out the door. Looking back, I saw this student was in tears. Knowing why, I walked back in and carefully approached her desk from one side as she busily wrote a book report. Leaning in close, I clicked the shutter several times so she'd hear it. There was no film in the camera, but she didn't know that, and when I left she looked very happy. Driving back to the newsroom after taking her picture, I felt I'd obeyed Mr. Gabriel's farewell wish to our class in Christian Science. "May it always be said of my pupils that they are sweet."

A few small honors came my way as readers recognized Monitor-style journalism in the Pilot-News. I hosted the Marshall County spelling bee finals one spring, and helped judge the Miss Maxinkuckee beauty contest that summer. And I landed a personal meeting with Bremen native Otis Bowen, recently retired as President Reagan's Secretary of Health and Human Services from 1985 to 1989.

Otis Bowen's Bremen neighbors all called him "Doc," since he had delivered many of them. After graduating from the Indiana University School of Medicine in 1942, he interned at Memorial Hospital in South Bend before serving in the Army Medical Corps during World War II. From 1946 until 1972, he practiced medicine in Bremen, delivering a whole generation of citizens known for years to come as Bowen babies.

In 1972 he began serving two consecutive terms as Governor of Indiana, and after eight years in the Governor's mansion, he was teaching at Indiana University when President Reagan picked him for a cabinet post. In 1989 he returned to his Bremen home, where I interviewed him.

Bowen told me Congress rarely responds to anticipated emergencies until they become immediate crises. Sadly,

Congress tends to allocate funds only when the need is urgent. In order to act as swiftly as possible, his department had to have plans prepared for immediate execution when funds finally became available.

At the end of our visit, as I rose to leave, Governor Bowen offered me a plastic bag filled with jelly beans he promised were from the Oval Office. Everyone knew President Regan loved jellybeans, or more precisely, Jelly Belly's, which have such delicate flavors the manufacturer recommends eating them one at a time, not by the handful. I took the Governor's gift back to the newsroom, giving one bean to each reporter on the staff. I wondered if they'd make us more conservative, but they had no effect.

After we arrived in Indiana from Massachusetts, Nicole could hardly believe the difference in her schoolmates. "The kids in the back two rows of some classes don't care if they fail or pass," she said incredulously. It was true. Some parents never graduated from high school, and didn't care if their children succeeded in class. They never stopped resenting school discipline.

After two years, her sister Michelle applied at Principia Upper School, a private boarding school for children who attended the Christian Science Sunday school. She immediately made new lifelong friends, and received the attention she deserved.

We wished Nicole would consider Principia too, but she seemed happy with her friends in Plymouth until one relationship went sour. Breaking up is hard to do, and she was still suffering when I slipped a note under the pillow on her bed. It said, "Did you ever notice that kids laugh when they graduate from Plymouth High, but when they graduate from Principia Upper School, they cry? Did you ever wonder why?"

The next morning, without commenting on my note, she came down to breakfast and announced, "I'm going to Principia. I'm not the smart one in the family, but I can draw."

Principia proved her wrong about not being smart. It happened the next Christmas when she came home for vacation with an assignment to write a paper on oriental tapestry. She did the research and wrote the paper, taking it back to campus in January, but the day it was due she accidentally left it in her dorm room.

Students could not return to the dorm during classes, so she assumed the teacher would ask her to present it the next day. But he didn't. He insisted she give it as scheduled. She told me later, "I remembered the first sentence of the paper, so I said that, and then I couldn't recall the rest, so I just told the class everything I knew about oriental tapestry. Her presentation earned her the first of many A's at Principia, and she graduated with honors. We were so grateful the teacher did not cut her any slack.

With both girls away at boarding school and heading soon for college, Evelyn earned her master's degree in secondary education and was hired as Director of Student Teaching at Indiana University South Bend. I would soon leave the Pilot-News for a new career, but not before one more opportunity to exhibit the Monitor's "problem- solving journalism" in Marshall County.

My phone rang one winter morning and a woman asked, "Are you the man who writes human interest stories?" "How human is it?" I joked. "I can't talk about it without crying," she said, so I agreed to come to her home in one hour.

She had a month-to-month lease on a farmhouse outside of town. She was a single mom with five children, and her youngest was a baby with a birth defect. He had to be monitored 24/7, and she wore a device on her belt to warn her if his heartbeat became irregular. A social worker came a few hours each week so she could leave the house and shop for groceries. She just received news that the house would be sold and she was being evicted. She'd called every apartment complex in town but none would rent to a family with five kids. Could the newspaper help? We were her last hope.

I pulled a chair over to the crib; stood up on it and aimed my camera down on the sick baby. Without delving into the whys or wherefores of missing fathers or a cruel landlord, I published her need on page one the next day under the headline, "Jimmy needs a home." As usual, the paper hit the streets at 3:00 p.m.

The next morning, I received a phone call from a wealthy reader of the newspaper. He owned a business in the industrial park, and offered me a deal. He would try to help this woman, if I let him do it in secret.

I agreed, and he had his attorneys investigate whether or not she would still be eligible for the free social worker she needed each week, if she owned real estate. They discovered she would be eligible for assistance if she owned a home. So he contacted her and asked her to find a home near town that would meet all her needs. After she found it, he would donate a down payment large enough that her mortgage payment would equal the amount she currently paid for rent. She did, and he did, and soon she was ready to move. But the blessing was not over yet.

A few days before she moved, the sisters at nearby Ancilla Convent called to ask if they could help. I mentioned that a new refrigerator and stove might be needed, and they provided both.

A few weeks later, I interviewed the mother again, at her new home. I asked her if she felt lucky. "With a baby on life support, I can't possibly feel lucky, she said, but I do feel blest." She said there was one aspect of the move that she still had not figured out. "Every few days, when I open the front door of my home to go outside, I find bags of groceries on the porch, and I have no idea where they come from."

Hearing this made me thankful to be "Back Home Again in Indiana," and helped me progress from reporting news about others to helping individuals one-on-one as a full-time Christian Science practitioner.

The Pilot-News, printed in Plymouth, is the only daily newspaper in Marshall County, Indiana. I wrote "human interest" stories for the paper that featured people, I hope, at their best and most interesting.

ༀ*15*

The Plain People

As a reporter for the Plymouth Pilot-News, I drove many miles throughout Marshall County in Indiana, and often passed slow-moving horse-drawn buggies. If I waved, the man or woman holding the reins always waved back, for this is the Amish way.

Something about these plain people endeared them to me, but they were not easy to befriend, since they were very private, so I prayed for an opening, and soon one appeared. An Amish man advertised in the newspaper for farm help, and included his name and postal address, since he had no telephone. I wrote immediately, explaining that I was not a farmer but would he like an "English" pen-pal? (Amish describe anyone who is not Amish as "English.") I watched my mailbox for a reply but none came, so after a few weeks I forgot about it.

Six months later I received a long chatty letter from someone with an unfamiliar name. He wrote as if we were old friends, explaining how he and other dads had just finished building a new one-room school for their children and hired a teacher. Suddenly it hit me. This was the Amish farmer I'd written to earlier, and he finally had time to welcome me as a pen-pal!

After we exchanged a few letters, I asked if I might visit the one-room school he helped build, and speak to the students. As a newspaper reporter, I could tell them the importance of reading and writing. When he asked the teacher, she agreed and a date was set. I had no idea what to expect as I drove into the driveway of that little Amish schoolhouse, nor did the students sitting inside. To them I might have been a man from the moon.

The school was designed with windows on the east and west

sides to allow as much sunshine as possible. Four overhead gas lamps waited to glow brightly on dark days, and a gas heater built into one wall promised warmth in the winter. Scholars in grades one through eight sat in straight rows facing the blackboard, learning from each other by answering in unison as the teacher gave a rapid-fire quiz. "How many days in a year? How many cups in a pint? Pounds in a ton? Quarts in a peck? Pecks in a bushel?"

Instead of a cafeteria, the school had a shelf near the door lined with lunch boxes, and once each week, on hot lunch day, a mother arrived at noon in her buggy bringing homemade pizza or some other treat. She might also bring a favorite blue beverage that the scholars jokingly called "Windex."

Each student paid quiet, respectful attention when I described my work as a journalist and explained why reading and writing are essential to success in life. As we said goodbye, I left some business cards behind in case any student wished to correspond with me. Several days later an envelope arrived with two letters written in pencil by two Amish sisters in the class. Their names were Lori and Marla, and their notes began a friendship that remains strong today. A few months later they invited me to their home for dinner and I met their two younger sisters, Emmalea and Verna, who were only five and six years old and could hardly speak English. (Amish speak Pennsylvania Dutch at home, and learn English in school.) I must have looked strange to them, but these shy preschoolers each took one of my hands and held it all evening, releasing me only to eat supper. In their white bonnets, they looked like Amish dolls named Purity and Innocence. After supper everyone remained at the table since chores were done and there was no television or computer beckoning from another room. All evening we sat at the table playing cards and singing hymns and telling jokes. And no matter how often I visited after that, their mother always prepared a homemade meal and sent me home with lots of leftovers.

During one visit, Lori offered to give me a ride in one of the family buggies, since she was old enough to drive the horse. We went around the block, which is exactly four miles in farm country. Marla sat in the back seat and I used the opportunity to ask questions. Were their church services very long? Yes. Did they ever feel bored in church? No! Why not? "Because we learn about the Bible," Lori said, "and I like to read it myself during the week." I asked her if she dropped the reins on the floor of the buggy, would the horse take her home anyway? She said yes, but it would not be safe, "because he cannot read the road sign that says 'Cross Traffic Does Not Stop.'" She almost had an accident one day for that very reason. She was reading her Bible while driving the buggy home from school and became so absorbed by a verse she found that she dropped the reins. The horse continued homeward, and was about to trot across a busy county road when she suddenly looked up, grabbed the reins and stopped him, probably saving her life. In retrospect, her close call reminds me of people today who text while driving. I don't suppose we need a law against reading the Bible while driving?

Before long, the children in this Amish family adopted me as their "English grandfather" and treated me like family. Lori and Marla were allowed to visit our home overnight and watch television, but insisted on preparing our meals and cleaning up afterward. They even let their hair down (literally) to show us how it hung almost to the floor. Only a trusted relative is ever allowed to see this, and we loved them as granddaughters.

One weekend a few years later, my stepdaughter Michelle and son-in-law Clay were in Indiana and came with Evelyn and me to visit the Amish. Clay custom-builds exquisite guitars from scratch and brought one of his instruments, leaving it in the car until the parents invited him to bring it inside. They asked him not to play it, since they never sing with instruments, but could he show it to them? The children crowded around eagerly as he unsnapped the case, and when he raised the lid, their eyes lit up as if the case held bars of gold. They said they'd never seen anything so beautiful, and finally their Dad asked, "Even if you don't play a song, could you just strum it so we can hear how it sounds?" Clay obliged, and the children were visibly thrilled, almost jumping up and down with excitement. It was a moment they remember to this day.

When I arrived for my final visit before we moved to North Carolina, the children ran out to the car to greet me, but their dad stayed inside. He wasn't feeling well, and needed to rest. It's hard to rest when six children are bouncing around the house, so I offered to drive them all to the general store a few miles away to buy ice cream for dessert. They were excited to go, and he was grateful for the quiet. As we drove away, I thanked God that each of His children is made in His image and likeness, as the Bible says. Not one is exhausted or uncomfortable, including the dad I left behind to get some rest.

When we arrived at the store, a sign in the window said "Shoes Required." The kids quickly offered to wait in the car, since they were all barefoot, but I went inside and asked the cashier if my Amish friends could come in too. He quickly agreed, and they had a wonderful time picking out the ice cream flavors their parents liked best. An hour went by, and when we returned to the farmhouse, their Dad greeted them at the door. He'd enjoyed a short nap and now he felt wonderful.

To me, the strangest thing about my Amish friends was how thankful they were for my friendship. I felt honored that they embraced me as family, but they felt equally honored that I treated their unique lifestyle with affectionate respect.

Since then, fifth-grade Marla has finished all eight years of Amish education. After graduation she worked two years as a clerk in a meat locker, and then began a career she continues today—as a teacher in a one-room school. Her sister Lori works with their dad in a nearby recreational vehicle factory. Little Emmalea and Verna will soon graduate from school and look for jobs. Emmalea is already earning a modest income knitting soft woolen caps for babies.

No one in the family is worried about their future. Perhaps they remember a sign that hung on the inside wall above the schoolhouse door. Its reassuring message promised, "One person can make a difference. Jesus did."

16

The public practice of Christian Science

*I*n the late 19th century, when Christian Science was still a new discovery, most adherents were attracted by physical healings they experienced or witnessed. Those who applied for the two-week course called "primary class instruction" used this training immediately to heal neighbors and friends through prayer alone. Some prayed for others only occasionally, but those who did this work full-time could advertise their names in the Christian Science Journal. The term "Journal-listed practitioner" does not constitute a personal church endorsement, but affirms advertisers have no other occupation and are available to help others 24/7.

By the time I received class instruction in 1970 from Charles Henry Gabriel, fewer "class-taught students" were becoming Journal-listed practitioners and there were obvious reasons for this change. Christian Science church congregations had been shrinking for twenty years. To fill vacancies on church committees, many members did church work almost full-time—conducting services, teaching Sunday school and serving on multiple committees while maintaining the edifice. In addition, some members who earned good salaries felt unable to surrender these for the modest incomes typically earned by practitioners. And others believed, even after taking class instruction, that they still did not know enough about Christian Science to pray for others. Each future practitioner takes an individual path, and mine was so modest that it began almost without my knowledge.

As a teen at summer camp, I felt sure God was present and could help anyone in trouble. One night a boy in a nearby cabin was coughing constantly. It was after Taps, and all the lights were off, but he kept coughing. Something told me to pray, and I remembered Jesus' words from the cross, "Father, forgive them for they know not what they do." I prayed this prayer, not for the coughing camper, but for myself. "Father, forgive my eyes for seeing things you never made, and forgive my ears for hearing sounds you never made, for they (my eyes and ears) know not what they do." I contemplated what God does see and hear—His own children, made in His perfect likeness with no uncomfortable ailments. Then I noticed it—silence. The coughing had stopped.

Did my prayer make a difference? Maybe the boy drank some water, or just fell asleep. I never felt responsible for his relief; just grateful for it, so imagine my surprise, fifty years later, when another former camper said she always felt I was a practitioner at camp. I asked if she had me confused with someone else, but she insisted, "No, there was a seriousness and sweetness about you, even as a boy."

Her fond memory awakened memories of the summer of 1965 when, as the senior counselor at camp, I was assigned to teach the CIT (counselor-in-training) Sunday school class. No one else wanted to teach it, because they felt teenagers are bored by religion. I asked God how to capture the interest of His children, how to feed His lambs, and a novel idea came to mind.

On the first Sunday of our summer together, the CITs and I sat in a circle on the sunny baseball field and I asked them for a favor—a vow of secrecy. Whatever was said in Sunday school stayed in Sunday school. They were perplexed, but finally agreed to keep our discussions top secret. Then, under our shield of secrecy, I asked if they really believed the Scientific Statement of Being is true.

The Scientific Statement of Being is a paragraph on page 468 of "Science and Health with Key to the Scriptures" by Mary Baker Eddy. It is "Christian Science in a nutshell," summarizing the bedrock principles of the faith, and is read at the end of every Christian Science Sunday church service, while the congregation remains standing. Since their parents accepted the statement as gospel, my CIT's assumed this was a trick question and hesitated to reply. I reminded them of the shield of secrecy, and gradually, one at a time, they each expressed sincere doubt about its veracity. Never before had they admitted this in Sunday school.

I welcomed their candor, because it would test a promise in the first verse of hymn 115 in our hymnal. "When we wandered, Thou hast found us; When we doubted, sent us light. . ." Would honest doubt really lead our class to the light of truth? To find out, I made a modest proposal. Would they join me in a secret study of the Scientific Statement of Being, to see if we could find even one grain of truth in it? Curious, they agreed and began a spiritual adventure that some would never forget.

According to the Scientific Statement of Being, there is no substance in matter, because God, Spirit, is All-in-all. But we knew there is matter. It's everywhere. So we found a rock and examined it. How big was it? The CITs agreed it was tiny to the eye of an elephant and huge to the eye of an ant. Did it feel the same to a bird and a termite? No. So who was right about the rock, the elephant or the ant or the bird or the termite, or us? Gradually they concluded the rock was mostly, perhaps entirely, in "the eye of the beholder," which is also the mind of the beholder, and if so, it might be an idea.

They were all surprised when I read these words from Mary Baker Eddy's "Miscellaneous Writings." "But, you say, is a stone spiritual? To erring material sense, No! but to un-erring spiritual sense, it is a small manifestation of Mind...." This was the first time Mrs. Eddy concurred with something they discovered on their own.

We didn't assume the Scientific Statement of Being is true. We debated it fearlessly, and not just in class. To bridge the gap between Sundays, each CIT wrote a confidential one-page paper for our class titled, "What God means to me this week that He did not mean last week." One student wrote, "In biology class our teacher told us man is made entirely of molecules, but that can't be true. Who ever heard of a funny molecule?" I kept each student's papers, and in the autumn, after camp had closed, mailed them to their homes as reminders of what we learned together.

No one broke our vow of secrecy that summer, even when a curious counselor teased that "nobody knows what happens in the CIT class." Why was the staff curious? Because they were noticing some very strange behavior.

CITs had one hour of free time each day, from four to five p.m. They guarded this hour carefully, but after a few weeks counselors noticed they were not playing tennis or volleyball during their free hour. Instead, they gathered in the pine grove to talk about (of all things) religion. Sunday school was never long enough to answer all their questions.

Near the end of August, a Christian Science lecturer named Lenore Hanks visited a nearby town to give a public talk for the local Christian Science church. Our camp hired two school busses and everyone went to hear her speak about "The Myth of Matter." She used many of the same examples CITs discussed in Sunday school. After the lecture, one CIT slapped me on the back and said knowingly, "That was right down our alley."

Today that CIT is an attorney with a Sunday school class of his own, where he uses some of the same illustrations we pondered at camp. A young lady in the class grew up to become superintendent of her church Sunday school. One day when I visited, she confided that ours was the best Sunday school class she ever had. The CITs taught me that Sunday school is wonderful preparation for the public practice of Christian Science, when God's fingerprints are on the lesson plan.

Along with taking primary class instruction, some who are preparing to be practitioners share inspiring ideas in church magazines. The weekly Christian Science Sentinel and its monthly companion, The Christian Science Journal, have published more than 30 of my contributions so far, including eleven poems, but I've never been a poet.

When he was an editor of the magazines, Peter Henniker-Heaton reviewed my first three poems and asked me to contribute more. He said the editors agreed my poetic style was perfect for sharing Christian Science. I admitted I wasn't a poet, and was as surprised as anyone when a verse came to mind. I never planned a poem, but every now and then I'd feel one "coming on," so I'd settle down and listen. The ideas for each verse always flowed naturally into thought. There was never a need to consider "what rhymes with what." It was like taking dictation. Two of my poems were reprinted in anthologies sold in Christian Science Reading Rooms, side-by-side with inspiring verses by "real" poets.

Some of my verses may have sounded romantic, but there was nothing ethereal about my articles. Most were based on lessons learned, usually the hard way. My first drafts were "written in blood," especially the one I wrote after my second divorce. Appropriately titled, "Healing Despair," it was written from a recently broken heart, and its no-nonsense bluntness touched another heart.

Mary Baker Eddy, who founded the church and its magazines, promised, "When the heart speaks, however simple. the words, its language is always acceptable to those who have hearts." ("Miscellaneous Writings," p. 262) I received two letters which prove she's right. The first came from a reader in Los Angeles, who wrote, "Your article, 'Healing Despair,' in the July 11, 1977, Sentinel has, I believe, saved me from absolute despair. The adequate words do not come with which to tell you how it has saved my sanity and my life. I am a life-long Christian Scientist and this article is bringing me back to joy and gladness. I am certain it was written for many others also, for this encouragement is much needed now."

The second letter arrived 37 years later, and was worth

waiting for. A young mother from Ojai, California, wrote, "Our daughter Katie is just seven. During the past year-and-a-half, she's had a favorite article, and it is by you. ('You are God's Peanut' from the June 25, 2012 Sentinel) She has asked me to read it to her well over 50 times. She likes that I almost cry when it comes to the part in the story about the melting ice cream. When she is feeling tender or a little scared, she asks me to read your article. She talks about who her shell is, and how to lean on God, and how God and parents are alike. One of the sweetest times was at a Wednesday evening testimony meeting at church. She picked up one of the free Sentinels in the hymnal rack and came across your peanut article. Her face just lit up, and she excitedly showed me the pages, like she had come upon an old friend."

During my first few years in the full-time practice of Christian Science, I was not yet listed in the Christian Science Journal. It seemed wise to first gain practical experience, and opportunities were plentiful. My first patient confided that her family business faced a crisis. She felt frustrated and anxious. She was not a church member, but asked me for prayerful support anyway. Afterward, she remembered, "Your manner was immediately reassuring and you provided some very helpful spiritual ideas for me to think about. Within a couple of days, a breakthrough was made toward resolving the problem and peace replaced my anxiety. I'm grateful for the prayerful support I received, and the turnaround that resulted from it."

A few months later, she asked me to pray for her daughter, who had an eye infection. She wrote later, "Her eye problem cleared up very quickly. We all appreciate your support."

A mom from a nearby city called to say her son lost his wallet. He was a student at Purdue University, and was in a bank when his billfold vanished. The bank let him view security video, but to no avail. Would I pray for him? Of course I agreed, reminding her that we don't have to believe anything is missing, since nothing is lost to God. We prayed

together and the next day the bank called her. They were trying to close the vault and the door would not seat properly.
When they inspected, they saw her son's wallet on top of the
door, preventing it from locking. Nothing was missing from
the billfold except $40, and the next week her son received a
$100 bonus check from his summer employer. His mom felt
this indicated the "completeness of the healing."

An elderly church member phoned seeking prayerful
help to relieve "irregularity and dizziness." She later recalled,
"You reminded me of Mary Baker Eddy's statement on page
283 of the textbook: 'Mind is the source of all movement,
and there is no inertia to retard or check its perpetual and
harmonious action.' I prayed with this idea, and by the
next morning I felt completely free. The problem has not
recurred since."

The mother of a teenage boy called asking for prayerful
help in his behalf. (Parents often call in behalf of their children.) He had a sore throat and was not sure if he could go
to school the next day. Later she recalled, "By the following
day his throat was better. I don't think he even realized how
quick his healing was, compared to how long others suffered
with the same problem."

A lady called for prayerful help after her dentist told her
she needed a tooth extracted and replaced by a bridge. She
and I prayed together for several days. She remembers, "The
pain stopped just before I went back for my second dental
visit. A new examination showed no extraction was needed.
The dentist said he must have been mistaken. He filled the
tooth and there has been no trouble since then."

By this time, my wife Evelyn and I had moved to Bloomington, Indiana, home of Indiana University, where she was
working on an advanced degree. For several years, members
of the Christian Science church in Bloomington maintained
a practitioner's office on the town square. None of the practitioners who served in the office were Journal-listed, but all
were eager to pray for anyone needing help. I gladly accepted

office hours two days a week, while teaching the college class in Sunday school.

As I sat in the well-appointed office listening for God's direction, a verse by 19ᵗʰ century hymn-writer Philip Bliss came to my thought. It says, "Dare to be a Daniel. Dare to stand alone! Dare to have a purpose firm! Dare to make it known." To me this felt like a signal from the Father to advertise my practice in the Christian Science Journal, but I still hesitated, until one more healing tipped the scale.

On Sunday, October 9, 1994, a first year student at the University of Maryland in College Park had a high fever. Her name was Vicky, and she grew up in the Christian Science Sunday school. I had prayed with her roommate in the past, so the roommate called me, holding the phone to Vicky's ear so we could speak together. Vicky said her high temperature, irritation and redness needed to be dealt with rationally and immediately. Later she remembered, "I listened openly to your calm reasoning and simple truths. You agreed to pray for me as long as I needed help. I fell asleep quietly reaffirming what you had told me and knowing that when I woke up all would be well. When I did awake the next morning, all the fever symptoms had vanished. This relief helped me feel God's presence and loving care. I went to my classes freely and shared this healing with others who witnessed my quick recovery and were amazed."

This proof of God's ever-present love was the encouragement I needed to apply for listing in the Christian Science Journal. My application was accepted, and Journal-listing opened even more doors to help others.

Meanwhile, three undergrads from Indiana University had been attending my Sunday school class each week. They were very different from the CITs at Camp Elektor. These students could ponder complexities like reductive materialism and we considered questions like, "If you had a microscope so powerful it could magnify an electron a million times, what would you see? Something? Or nothing? And why?" Even without a vow of secrecy, these older students hungered for simple truths that set us all free from fear and discord.

One Sunday I challenged them to quit thinking about God, and try thinking as God, for at least a moment or two each day. They were intrigued, and they were almost sure they could do it. Then one student actually did. He told us the next Sunday that he was walking down a concrete outdoor stairway at his dorm one morning holding some books when he tripped. The books went flying and he tumbled down five steps to the landing below. He felt shocked and unsure if he could stand up, and as he sat there he decided to quit thinking about God, and try thinking as God. What would God think about him right now? The Bible says God made man in His image and likeness, so God could not know him as fallen, since God cannot fall. God could not know him as shocked or hurt, because God is never shocked or hurt. God could not know him as a victim of passing time, because God is eternal, not temporal. God could only know the truth about him—his uninterrupted perfection and God-like harmony.

He told us he suddenly realized he felt okay. He stood up easily, collected his books, and continued to class with no after-effects from an accident that never happened in the mind of God. Later he wrote me, "Not only did you help solve my individual problem, but you offered solutions to many human needs I will encounter in the future. You helped lead me along the right path, and for that I'll always be grateful."

Advertising one's name, postal address, phone number and email address in the practitioner directory of the Christian Science Journal may not designate official endorsement by the church, but it enables strangers to request prayerful help from a distance. If an article or poem in a church magazine resonates with someone anywhere in the world, they may search the practitioner directory in each issue of the Journal for the author's name. The first person to contact me after finding my name in the Journal was a lady from Boston. She had been a regular participant on a television program where the Christian Science Weekly Bible Lesson was read, and she now sought new employment. One of my articles inspired her, so she asked for prayerful support. I was in Indiana, but she knew distance is no barrier to prayer, since God is everywhere. In a few days she sent this note. "Thank you for your letter and your prayers. I have a small piece of paper on my desk with the words you gave me when we spoke on the phone, 'Christ is in control, and only good can result.' I am already seeing positive results, and am grateful for your prompt, effective prayers."

Full-time practitioners may also receive invitations to give inspirational talks. In January, 1997, I was invited to give a chapel talk to the students at the Principia Upper School in St. Louis. The co-ed, K-12 private boarding school, which our daughters had attended, is open to children from all over the world who attend the Christian Science Sunday school. The talk was only 10 minutes long, between breakfast and first period classes, and since many of the students were teenagers, I answered the unspoken question on everyone's mind, "How Can I Find Mr. or Miss Right?" I shared how I was healed of loneliness by looking for God's face in everyone I met, and encouraged all who felt lonely to try this in the hallway as soon as chapel ended. Students paid close attention, and the school principal later wrote, "We so appreciated the clear message to our students about their true, divine nature." But this chapel talk had an unforeseen side effect.

The principal's mother could not attend, so he gave her a tape recording to enjoy. She wrote, "I had been having some trouble hearing out of one ear, and had been praying for relief. I had to talk on the telephone using the other ear for several days. When I picked up the recorder and inadvertently held it to my deaf ear, I heard your talk perfectly. I truly appreciate the benefit it gave me."

Another invitation came to speak informally at the Christian Science church in Vincennes, Indiana. Like congregations of many denominations, their membership was declining and they feared it might be necessary to disband. Could I share a few encouraging words? It was an honor to remind them of something an experienced practitioner told me years before. He said that if church has any enemy, it is the beguiling suggestion that church includes degrees of sin. But holy inspiration disallows this. Christ's church is sinless. In church, grace can never becomes disgrace, nor can honor become dishonor. All identities in church glorify God, and we are surely among them. In church we have the joy of treading where the saints have trod, and the inspiration that made their faces shine can be seen in ours.

I asked no fee for my talk, but the members insisted I take several bags of juicy fresh peaches from their orchards. One member wrote later, "Spirituality permeated the whole event. I was astounded at the number of people there, including some non-members. Everyone was in a mood of quiet receptivity." At this writing, the church in Vincennes is still active.

When class instruction from Charles Henry Gabriel ended in 1970, it was followed by his annual association meeting, a day when everyone in every class returned to hear our teacher share an inspirational address. Association meetings are spiritual reunions, reminding us what we learned in class. So what happens to an association after the teacher of Christian Science dies and can no longer give the talk? Often an executive board is appointed to invite guest speakers recommended by members of the association. These speakers are almost always practitioners listed in the Christian Science Journal.

I never expected to receive such an invitation, but in April, 1997, the Association of the Pupils of Katheryn McCord Watt of Chicago had a last-minute cancellation. Their executive board was at a loss, and called a practitioner they knew well. Could she speak at the last minute? Sadly, she could not, but she mentioned me. No one on the executive board had ever heard of me, but because of her recommendation, they sent an invitation and I accepted.

A typical association address is four hours long—two hours in the morning and two in the afternoon. It's about 230 typed pages, double-spaced. This meeting was only eight weeks away, so I had to pray fast and listen closely for God's guidance. Fortunately I'd heard outstanding addresses from Mr. Gabriel, so I knew what the pupils of Mrs. Watt needed and deserved to hear. Solid conviction. Profound, familiar truths presented in a fresh ways. And of course, humor.

The association met at the Executive House hotel in downtown Chicago. None of the pupils could play a piano, so they had not sung a hymn for many years, but Evelyn changed that. She brought her keyboard and we sang four hymns during the day.

My subject was the 23rd Psalm, and I treated it like a Christmas tree, decorating each branch (or verse) with spiritual lessons, healing stories and anecdotes designed to bring out deeper spiritual meanings.

As the fourth hour was about to end, we all recited the final verse together. "Surely goodness and mercy shall follow me all the days of my life, and I will dwell in the house of the Lord forever." I closed with a reassuring promise, wrapped in this humorous story.

"Mary Smith's little boy Jimmy was about to begin first grade. She wanted to walk him to school, but he said he was a big boy and wanted to walk with his buddy, Tommy, who lived next door. Tommy was starting second grade and knew the way to school. Jimmy's Mom consented, but she was still afraid he and Tommy might get lost because they were so young. So she called her friend Cynthia down the street. Cynthia just had a baby, and walked her through the neighborhood in a stroller each day. Would Cynthia mind walking some distance behind Jimmy and Tommy when they went to school, just to be sure they arrived safely? Cynthia promised to walk far enough back that she would not be noticed, but one day Tommy asked Jimmy if he knew the name of the lady following them with a stroller? Jimmy said yes. 'Well, who is it?' Tommy asked. 'I'm pretty sure it's Shirley Goodnest and her daughter Marci,' Jimmy said. 'What makes you think that?' 'Because every night my Mom makes me repeat the 23rd Psalm before bed, and it says Shirley Goodnest and Marci shall follow me all the days of my life, so I just have to get used to it.'"

As we parted that afternoon, I reminded the students to look over their shoulder if they ever feel worried or upset. "Shirley Goodnest and Marci are never far behind."

That evening, after walking Chicago's Magnificent Mile, Evelyn and I stayed overnight in the Executive House, and the next morning, as we prepared for breakfast, the phone rang in our room. It was the secretary of the Watt association. "Your talk reminded us so much of our teacher," she said, "Would you come back in a few years and speak to us again?" I gratefully agreed, and in my heart I hoped Mrs. Butterworth felt her secret investment in my childhood was paying the dividends she hoped for.

I returned to address the Watt association one more time, and other invitations followed: one from an association in Indianapolis and two more from an association in Louisville. Soon after my second address in Louisville, I accepted an invitation to serve as co-administrator of Midland House, a non-medical care facility in Indianapolis open to anyone seeking healing through the study of Christian Science. The administrative work was closely aligned with spiritual healing, and the Christian Science Journal originally permitted listed practitioners to do this work. But that policy had changed, so I stopped advertising in the Journal in order to help save Midland House from drowning in red ink.

༄17

Midland House

O n July 27, 1909, Mary Baker Eddy sent a letter to the directors of her church in Boston, asking them to "establish and maintain a Christian Science resort for the so-called sick." A few weeks later, she wrote again, saying she was willing to let the matter rest for a while, but it was never forgotten, and in 1919 the directors opened a large Christian Science care facility in Chestnut Hill, near Boston. It was called The Christian Science Benevolent Association, and was staffed by Christian Science nurses. The title "Christian Science nurse" may sound contradictory until one knows exactly what services a non-medical nurse offers.

Christian Science nurses provide skilled bedside care on a basis consistent with the teachings of their religion. This requires sufficient practical wisdom to ensure a patient's comfort, rest, cleanliness, safety, mobility and nourishment. Christian Science nurses are also trained to dress wounds, as needed. They are not trained or permitted to diagnose illness or give a patient medicine.

As her church's membership grew, Mrs. Eddy knew some who were seeking healing through prayer alone would need the tender attention of a nurse who shared their trust in God. Among Christian Science nurses, attitude is as important as aptitude. "An ill-tempered, complaining or deceitful person should not be a nurse," writes Mrs. Eddy. "The nurse should be cheerful, orderly, punctual, patient, full of faith, —receptive to Truth and Love." In the Church Manual, she specifies that "A member of The Mother Church who represents himself or herself as a Christian Science nurse shall be one who has a demonstrable knowledge of Christian

Science practice, who thoroughly understands the practical wisdom necessary in a sick room, and who can take proper care of the sick."

The Christian Science Benevolent Association in Chestnut Hill, Massachusetts (later known as the Chestnut Hill Benevolent Association) was the first religious, non-medical healthcare institution staffed by Christian Science nurses, but many more followed, serving patients in different parts of the world. One of these was Midland House, in Indianapolis, Indiana.

When Midland House first opened in the 1950s, it was filled to capacity and there was a waiting list. Each patient received prayerful support from a Christian Science practitioner, along with Christian Science nursing care, and many healings were recorded.

The daughter of one patient remembers: "We lived in Indianapolis while my mother resided in Anderson. One day I received a call from my mother's sister saying I needed to come home at once because my mother had a stroke and was unconscious and unable to move. Anderson is only 35 miles from Indianapolis, and when I got there, I called a Christian Science teacher in Indianapolis and asked her to pray for my mother. She agreed to pray, but strongly urged me to call an ambulance and have mother taken to Midland House. I asked why, and the practitioner said, 'You want her to get well, don't you? The nurses will encourage her to do whatever she can for herself, even if it's just pulling the sheet up a bit.' That day I watched mother being carried into Midland House on a stretcher, still unconscious and unable to move. Six weeks later, she walked out the door completely healed. After staying four months with us, she got her own apartment and lived on her own for several years, driving her grandchildren to school, piano lessons and sports events."

Eventually Christian Science churches in Indiana grew smaller, and Midland House had only a handful of patients, mostly receiving long-term elder care. The facility had been in debt for years, sending frequent appeals to church members for financial aid. When the Midland board asked me to serve as administrator, Midland was (again) on the verge of financial collapse, despite a dedicated staff. My co-administrator, Lyn Anderson, had previous served on the Executive Board and was devoted to Christian Science nursing. He knew all the "nuts and bolts" of the physical plant, and loved every patient like family. By working in close coordination, he and I returned Midland House to solvency within 18 months.

As we prayed, Lyn and I realized the true need was not more money, but more love. We remembered Mrs. Eddy's admonition in the Church Manual that "God requires wisdom, economy and brother love to characterize all the proceedings of the members of The Mother Church, the First Church of Christ, Scientist." And we pondered the question the prophet Elisha asked the poor widow, "What has thou in the house?" (see II Kings, 4:1-6)

As a result of prayer and listening, we felt inspired to place a sign on the administrator's office door that said, "Kindness spoken here." We cherished the hard-working, unselfish staff and helped them in every possible way. A few staff members who noticed this sign came to our office to express appreciation. We also vowed to stop sending out financial appeals, and to better appreciate each unsolicited contribution. Then we noticed that for many years Midland's corridors had been adorned with exquisite oil paintings. No one remembered where the paintings came from, so we had them appraised and several were very valuable. These were sold and replaced by new, more affordable art. Patients enjoyed the change, and income from the sale enabled us to reduce the deficit.

A few months later, we re-evaluated a corner parcel of wooded land behind our nursing residence. It faced the road and was not needed, so we hired a realtor to sell it, and funds from the sale erased all debt and enabled some needed improvements.

Lyn and I were both hired on an "interim" basis, and after 18 months we asked the board to replace us. After a nationwide search, they found an applicant who was not only a Christian Science nurse, but also an attorney. He was hired, and we gratefully gave him the keys to a facility with a balanced budget.

Midland House opened at this site on E. 56th Street in Indianapolis in the summer of 1976. It was a pleasure working with Mrs. Kathy McMullen, Superintendent of Christian Science Nursing shown here with me. After meeting the needs of many patients, Midland House closed and was sold in 2010.

18

Return to the "Fourth Estate"

With Midland House finally solvent, I was prepared to resume the public practice of Christian Science. Then our local newspaper, the Herald-Times of Bloomington, Indiana, where we lived, advertised for a general assignment reporter. Priceless memories of years at the Christian Science Monitor and the Plymouth Pilot-News beckoned me to rejoin the Fourth Estate. Others had already applied, but I was offered the job and gratefully accepted, spending the next five years obedient to the Monitor's motto, "to injure no man and bless all mankind."

Initially my story assignments were routine—reporting on police rescue divers as they practiced in frigid wind on ice-covered Lake Monroe, or interviewing a mechanic who built a pneumatic cannon with a barrel 30 feet long from which he could shoot a pumpkin faster than the speed of sound (I watched one of his supersonic pumpkins penetrate the door of a Pontiac parked in a distant field), or discussing culinary art with residents of nearby Martinsville who baked the world's largest apple pie on the town square, and cut it into 5,000 servings.

Former Speaker of the U.S. House of Representatives Tip O'Neill is remembered for saying, "All politics is local," and the same is true of news. The more local a story, the more timeless it becomes. With this in mind, I prayed for guidance before calling schools in rural towns where the Herald-Times circulated to ask if they had any "breaking news." Field trips to the zoo or upcoming dance parties were rarely covered, but sometimes my prayerful outreach produced meaningful results.

One morning, for example, I called the principal of Gosport Elementary School and was told about a student initiative to expand the library following the death of a child named David Wellman. The story was so inspiring that I drove to Gosport and interviewed the student council president, sixth-grader Danielle Jones. She said David died of illness "two years ago, after finishing third grade." Ever since he learned to read, he loved books, and after his death a special bookcase in the library was dedicated in his memory. Parents and friends donated new and used books, but the library still had half-empty shelves.

"We think the library needs more books," Danielle told me, "so we decided to sell suckers that change color as you suck them. We allowed students to go to the gym and read a book for 25 cents." A bake-sale also raised funds for the library. "Moms did most of the baking," she admitted, "and we made over $300 in three days." To raise more funds, the student council recommended kids be allowed to wear hats to school if they donated 25 cents to the book fund. The principal wore an oversize cowboy hat.

How much did students collect during their week-long campaign? School secretary Barb Dunigan's desk was covered with pennies, nickels and dimes as she tallied the total. "They raised $346.25," she concluded, "all to buy books that David liked," and she was touched the Herald-Times cared enough to send a reporter to interview their Student Council president on the playground during afternoon recess. Returning to the newsroom, I knew this story would be clipped from the paper and gently placed in family albums for posterity. I could hardly believe I was paid to share such good news. It wasn't work. It was an honor. And it became a greater honor when His Holiness the Dalai Lama of Tibet came to town.

The 1999 Kalachakra for World Peace featured 11 days of interfaith teaching by the Dalai Lama at the Tibetan Cultural Center in south Bloomington. Daily admission was $50, or $40 for students, seniors and Tibetans. And why did His Holiness come to Bloomington, instead of New York

City or San Francisco? Because of family. His older brother, Thubten Norbu, fled from Tibet to America in 1965 and made his way to Bloomington where he became a professor at Indiana University, guiding the school's Tibetan studies program. In 1979 he opened the Tibetan Culture Center, which was patrolled by city, county and state police during the Dalai Lama's visit.

Buddhist teachings about world peace would surely be inspiring, but first everyone had to get past U.S. State Department security. One agent told me, "President Clinton sent us to protect the Dalai Lama because he is considered a foreign dignitary."

Kalachakra faithful passed through a metal detector before approaching the inner grounds. Guests in vehicles had to step outside and be scanned by electronic wands while agents used mirrors on long poles to examine the bottom of each car for bombs. Reporters from as far away as the South China Morning Post placed costly cameras on the lawn where a dog wearing a blue "Explosives K-9" collar eagerly sniffed each open equipment bag. To keep the dogs alert, officers would "plant" an explosive in one of the bags. When the dog caught the scent, he signaled by sitting beside the bag and refusing to move until given a doggie treat.

After gaining entry, we all strolled along a wooded path to the Teaching Tent, a temporary steel frame about the size of an airplane hangar, covered with white fabric. Inside, 5,000 wooden folding chairs formed a vast semi-circle facing a wall of colorful sacred paintings for meditation, drawn on silk. Small flags fluttered overhead, moved by the cool breeze of air-conditioners in the back of the tent.

A few faithful tried to balance barefoot in the lotus position on folding chairs, but most just relaxed after partially prostrating themselves to the Lama—touching their head, throat and heart with both hands while holding palms together. A monk explained this gesture to me. He said the head symbolizes the body, the throat symbolizes speech, and the heart symbolizes the mind, showing the Buddhist desire to serve the Lama with body, speech and mind.

Everyone stood up when His Holiness slowly entered the tent and took his seat at a beautifully draped table. Monks opened the meeting with a chant, and then he began speaking in Tibetan, pausing every few minutes while a translator repeated his teaching in English.

Among other things, he explained that the Kalachakra deity includes no matter. "We pay homage to a deity whose first quality is compassion," he said, adding that "everyone has the ability to attain the highest state of Kalachakra, but what obstructs us from fulfilling our full potential? Pollutants of the mind, mental and emotional afflictions, are factors that need to be purified."

During the Dalai Lama's two-week visit, Bloomington was crowded with tourists and Buddhist monks in saffron robes, including Matthieu Ricard, a monk who sometimes served as the Dalai Lama's interpreter. Speaking at the local Barnes and Noble Booksellers, he described how Buddhists meditate.

"Meditation is more than sitting under a mango tree in India with an empty mind," he said with a smile. "It's a process of gradual transformation; a new way of seeing things. You might meditate on a quality you wish to develop, such as compassion. Compassion is the wish to free beings from suffering and the causes of suffering. This wish is directed toward sentient beings, but also toward enlightenment and wisdom. Without wisdom about how ignorance brings suffering, you cannot help anyone, not even yourself. Compassion must be cultivated through meditation until it has intensity. Behind what might initially look like exotic forms, the Buddhist path is designed to help us become better human beings."

When I asked him to summarize his faith in one word, he said, "It's really about love."

During the next few years, I was grateful to cover events

featuring well-known speakers like Senator Elizabeth Dole, Senator Richard Lugar, singer John Mellencamp and General Colin Powell, whose comments were always front page news. It's easy to report anything that's "big and fearful," but I prayed to find stories about the "small and tearful," and this prayer was answered when I met Donna Hardway. Many years earlier, as a six-year-old girl, she was the youngest Munchkin in the cast of the 1939 movie, "The Wizard of Oz," and her story was surprising.

Hardway told me her career began when she won a baby contest at age three. Soon afterward she joined the Meglin Kiddies, a showcase for Hollywood child stars including Shirley Temple, Judy Garland, Mickey Rooney and Ann Miller.

As a Meglin Kiddie, she sang and danced for wounded World War I soldiers at a Los Angeles hospital before her agent, Susan Carroll (who later married Alan Ladd) helped her join the cast of "The Wizard of Oz." Did she enjoy it?

"It was the most frightening thing I've ever been through!" she said. "It was the biggest sound stage I'd ever been on. It was so noisy, with people yelling and hollering and joking and running around. It was bedlam."

She said the cast included 124 adult "little people" but more Munchkins were needed, so she and 10 other "normal size" youngsters served as extras with no speaking roles. They were mostly visible as tiny arms waving through windows. Hardway had difficulty relating to adult "little people" in the cast, since they were her exact height but decades older. "A lot of them had beards," she said, "and they smoked and cursed. It was very confusing to me."

Hardway never watched the movie until she saw it with her own children in the 1950s. For many years she ignored Oz festivals because she felt she was "just part of the scenery," but when I met her, she had embraced Oz fans as family, since "I was in the film, and I was the youngest of all."

During my years with the Christian Science Monitor,

reporters and correspondents were directed to never leave the reader hopeless, but always include a possible solution in each problem or tragedy. This problem-solving approach was not Pollyanna optimism, but simply a focus on positive facts. If other newspapers headlined a story, "Ten Die in Plane Crash," the Monitor headline might read, "Three Survive Plane Crash."

For students of Christian Science, prayer is almost a knee-jerk reaction to any form of evil. If something is unfair, unjust, or potentially fatal, it cannot come from a God who is love. And if God, divine Love, is everywhere, then should we dread evil? Poet Edgar Guest answered this question in a verse called "Fear," which says in part:

> *The great god Fear grinned back at me;*
> *"I am the foe men never see,*
> *The hurt they never feel," said he.*
> *"I have no voice and yet I speak;*
> *No strength and yet I blanch the cheek*
> *And leave the strongest mortals weak.*
> *I am man's cruelest, bitterest foe,*
> *Yet past his door I could not go,*
> *Had he the wit to tell me: 'No'."*
>
> (Collected Verse of Edgar A. Guest, The Reilly & Lee Co., Chicago, 1945)

These thoughts were on my mind when I was assigned to interview a 69-year-old Indiana University English professor emeritus named Jim Jensen. He was in the beginning stages of renal failure and needed a kidney transplant within four months to avoid dialysis. Because of his age, he was not eligible for a kidney from a live donor list, and cadaver transplants were reserved for patients already on dialysis. Doctors believed Jensen would be too ill to qualify for any transplant after five years on dialysis. He needed to find a living donor soon who had type A or O positive blood, was in good health, and was not a public safety officer like a policeman or firefighter. My article ended hopefully with a telephone number for qualified donors to call, and an unspoken prayer that God, divine Love, meets every human need and could not overlook Jim Jensen. One year later, almost to the day, I learned what subsequently happened.

According to an article by fellow reporter Dann Denny, Jensen's wife sent dozens of letters to friends and relatives about her husband's dire need. Then the Indiana University Alumni Association made a mass appeal in his behalf to 70,000 people. As a result, 17 volunteered to be tested as possible donors. Sixteen were Jensen's personal friends or family members. The seventeenth, who was ultimately chosen by doctors as the best donor, was Susan Dabkowski of Bloomington, a complete stranger. But why would Dabkowski offer to donate a kidney to a man she never met? She claimed it was the story I wrote about Jensen's urgent need.

"As I read the story," she said, "it was as if Jim's guardian angel tapped me on the shoulder and said, 'Pay attention. You're the one.' As I read, I was touched in a way I can't explain logically. When I finished it, I clipped it out and placed it on the kitchen table. There was an inner nudging that would not let me throw it away."

A week later, she read the story again and noticed one of the blood types Jensen needed was O positive. "That leaped off the page," she said. "I'm O positive," so she called the number in the newspaper and threw herself into the ring as a possible donor. After five months of tests, Jensen received one of Dabkowski's healthy kidneys and a new lease on life.

Family members said that, after the transplant, he seemed happier than he'd been in years, laughing at the drop of a hat and wearing an irrepressible smile.

"What's amazing about this whole thing," he said, "is that my life was saved by a total stranger," claiming Dabkowski gave him "a happy kidney" because her personality bubbles. In a thank-you note to her, he wrote, "Your magnificent gift not only gave me my true love back and allowed us to grow old together. It also returned something I lost a long time ago—hope." His note moved Dabkowski to tears, and as I read it, I understood better what "problem solving journalism" can accomplish when supported by prayer.

Among many helpful features, the Herald-Times had a consumer column called "Hotline." As time went by, it deteriorated into a gray newsroom orphan, rotated among any disinterested reporters who had a few spare moments to answer reader questions. When our sister-newspaper, the South Bend Tribune, upgraded their consumer complaint column, the editor asked if I could make Hotline as good as the Trib. After I promised to make Hotline much better than the Trib, I became the exclusive Hotline columnist.

Thanks to the Internet, it was easy to answer most reader questions, so I added unexpected humor, inventing a mystery vehicle called the Hotmobile in which I allegedly drove around town investigating reader complaints. The fictional vehicle was serviced by a fictional Hotmobile pit crew and became so popular with readers that the editor ordered two large magnetic signs for the doors of my Toyota which said, "Herald-Times Hotmobile." Within a year Hotline became a "read me first" feature among seniors at area retirement homes who discussed each question and answer over lunch. A few weeks before Christmas, The Herald-Times general manager "tested" the new column by asking anonymously if the Santa Claus in Macy's Thanksgiving Day parade had a real beard. I called the store and printed their answer verbatim. "Of course our Santa has a real beard. That's because he's the real Santa. Didn't you see the movie 'Miracle on 34th Street'?"

To supplement a steady stream of consumer complaints, I visited local elementary schools and spoke to older classes, describing Hotline and inviting them to submit questions. One child from a parochial school wrote to ask, "Is there music in heaven?" Hotline answered yes, reminding him,

"Hark, the herald angels sing!"

Hotline was accurate, clever and sometimes funny, but did it have any spiritual value? I wasn't sure, so I asked God to show me how a consumer complaint feature could have a divine influence on the lives of readers. That's when a letter arrived from a single mother in nearby Springville. She wrote, "My 16-year-old daughter recently spent her life savings of $1,400 on a car. She bought it from the director of a local mission who said he used the money to help fund the mission. Less then two miles down Indiana 37, the engine locked up. It will cost $2,500 to make it run. Is there a lemon law, or something my daughter can do to get her money back? For me, this experience gives a sad slant on the acronym WWJD (What would Jesus do?)."

To me, the obvious question concerned a car, but the hidden question concerned values. A quote from a Christian Science practitioner came to mind. He said, "If matter matters most to me, then matter's the matter with me!" I replied by pointing out that unless the car had less than 1,800 miles, it was exempt from Indiana's Vehicle Protection Act, or lemon law. Then I addressed the hidden question by quoting Olympic gold medalist Wilma Rudolph, who said we should "never underestimate the power of dreams and the influence of the human spirit." I encouraged her daughter to contact the man who sold her the car and tell him what happened, remembering that "the man you speak to is the man who will answer," so give him the benefit of the doubt. As I published this reply, I truly loved this mother and her daughter and the man who sold the car.

Two weeks later, the mother wrote again, recalling her earlier question and my answer. She continued, "What happened next restored my faith in humanity. Another Hotline reader contacted you asking to help my daughter. You sent us her phone number and we called her. She offered to give my daughter $2,000 to fix her car! My daughter declined the gift since she had not earned it, but told this wonderful woman about one of her friends who is training for mission-ary work in India and needs financial support. This reader agreed to contribute $500 toward the friend's expenses. The matter of the car was just dropped. We've invited this kind reader lady to our house to visit. We have a big garden and my daughter wants to give her flowers and vegetables. I've learned that money comes and goes, but real friendship with genuine people is priceless."

Hotline replied, "We encouraged your daughter to never underestimate the power of dreams, and the influence of the human heart. Apparently she took this advice, because her unselfishness transformed a loss which was hard to forget into a gift she'll always remember."

My career as Hotline reporter at the Herald-Times could have continued many years, but in May, 2006, I was invited to resume full-time church work by serving as media and legislative liaison for all Christian Science churches in the state. The official title was Christian Science Committee on Publication for Indiana, and it felt like a divine calling, so I bid goodbye to readers in a final Hotline column which said, "It's been fun meeting you here each weekday for the past few years, but new work beckons, so I must surrender the quill I plucked from the goose that laid the golden egg called Hotline. Now it's time to crank the Hotmobile one last time, climb aboard and chug off into the sunset. On behalf of my trusty assistant, Dorothy 'Dot' Google, and the entire Hotmobile pit crew, I bid you all a loving farewell."

The Herald Times building in Bloomington, Indiana, Christmas, 2015. Photo by Lauren Slavin.

❧ 19

Committee on Publication for Indiana

*A*fter Mary Baker Eddy published her textbook and began teaching others to heal through prayer, many false and hostile articles about Christian Science appeared in the public press. To correct this misinformation, she created a three-man Publication Committee in 1885. Early in 1900 she formalized the work with Article XXXIII in the Church Manual establishing a one-man Committee of Publication in Boston who would manage similar one-man committees in each state and nation where Christian Science churches existed. In 2006, I was appointed to fill this role in Indiana. My duty, as defined in the Church Manual, was "to correct in a Christian manner impositions on the public in regard to Christian Science, injustices done Mrs. Eddy or members of this church by the daily press, by periodicals or circulated literature of any sort." Circulated literature included proposed bills in state legislatures that limited anyone's freedom to practice Christian Science.

Committees are paid by a per capita tax accessed on each church member in his or her state, and as time went by some members began viewing their Committee as an unofficial "bishop" who could resolve disagreements over church procedure. Committees received questions like, "May we hold a funeral in our church?" or "May we serve lunch after a Sunday service?" Committee decisions were considered binding until, by the time I was appointed, the original purpose of Committee work was clarified and such questions were no longer answered. Individual branch churches were expected to solve their own problems, address their own issues based on Mrs. Eddy's insistence that branch churches be independent, the Church Manual's stipulations, and their own common sense.

State Committees were supported by volunteer Assistant Committees in each church in their jurisdiction. These assistants scanned local newspapers daily for mistakes about Christian Science and, for many decades, such media misinformation was quickly corrected, until a day arrived when state Committees received both good and bad news.

Christian Science had apparently dropped off media radar, and was rarely mentioned unjustly by the press. That was the good news. As a result, state Committees on Publication had less to do. That was the bad news.

Managers in Boston, who changed every few years, created fresh initiatives to keep state Committees active. At one time, Committees supervised statewide programs in which Assistant Committees placed copies of the Christian Science textbook and biographies of Mary Baker Eddy in local public libraries. One year, Committees helped sell the trade edition of "Science and Health with Key to the Scriptures" at book fairs and mind-body-spirit conferences. Even with these projects, many state Committees spent hours in their offices waiting for the phone to ring, but soon after my appointment, all that changed.

With the dawn of social media, a forward-looking Manager in Boston directed all state Committees to move their offices into their cars and hit the road in a campaign to meet face-to-face and create a personal relationship with every legislator and editor in their state as soon as possible. Why? Because studies found that many legislators and editors had never met a Christian Scientist in their life, and when faced with a bill or news story mentioning the church, they had no idea how to respond. If they knew the state Committee personally, they might call him, and avoid future mistakes based on misinformation. In an understatement, this new duty was described as "not your grandfather's Committee work."

This initiative presented a unique challenge in Indiana. My predecessor had served as Committee for more than 20 years. Beloved by church members statewide, he had one fault that he freely admitted. He could not throw anything away. When I first visited his office on Monument Circle in Indianapolis, the doorway was partially blocked by surplus office furniture including at least six tall filing cabinets stuffed with files dating back to 1920. My first assignment —to purge the files and vacate the office—was impossible without divine guidance, so I asked God for helpful ideas, and then listened.

Fortunately, my years working for the Christian Science Monitor helped me identify the few files with historic value. Countless bags of needless files were shredded and discarded. Surplus books were given to charity and barrister bookcases were sold to an antique dealer. Then God's fingerprints became apparent.

I had advertised the five-foot high office safe in the building tenants' magazine, and the owner of a pizza parlor on the first floor bought it immediately. Then another tenant asked if I had anything else to sell. He ran a social service agency on the third floor and I invited him to see the worthless old desks, chairs and empty cabinets that remained. He could not believe his eyes. "If you want to sell everything, I can use it all," he said. "I have clients who urgently need used furniture and this would really bless them." I offered everything to him for free if he would haul it away. His movers soon arrived, and when they left, the office was bare. Even dented trash cans and cracked old plastic mats under desk chairs were gone. When only the carpet remained, I was able to cancel the lease, return the keys to the landlord, and follow my Manager's direction to "hit the road." I could hardly believe it happened so swiftly in a way that helped others.

Committees on Publication are inspired by a promise in "Science and Health," where Mrs. Eddy writes, "The sunlight glints from the church-dome, glances into the prison-cell, glides into the sick chamber, brightens the flower, beautifies the landscape, blesses the earth."

Sunlight often symbolizes truth, and Committees know truth glints from the church-dome for reflection but never lingers there like an idle halo. It's in perpetual motion, glinting, glancing, gliding, brightening, beautifying and blessing.

While serving as Committee for Indiana, I saw truth "brighten the flower," as I answered questions from individual lawmakers and editors about Christian Science, and watched it beautify "the landscape" while satisfying collective curiosity about spiritual healing among college students in a comparative religion class at the University of Indianapolis.

The class welcomed representatives from several religions each semester. During my visit, I quickly discovered nobody knew the name Mary Baker Eddy, and none had ever heard the false rumor that Christian Science forbids medical care, but they did know our church prints a "good newspaper." After our visit a dozen students accepted gift copies of "Science and Health." One said she believed all religions have unique merits. I told her that is "buffet theology" and I hoped she'd take a big serving of Christian Science. She replied sweetly, "Maybe I'll make Christian Science the cherry on my dessert."

The following winter I attended an all-day conference on Healing through Prayer at Earlham College in Richmond, Indiana. Almost 100 people from many faiths told why they believed prayer cured them. One lady said she was gravely ill and prayed to know if she would die. What came to mind totally surprised her. She felt she would not die, "but I'd have to fight for my health." She said she knew nothing about spiritual combat and could only remember a cheer from her years at Muncie Central High School. So even though it seemed foolish, she prayed over and over to God, "Fight! Fight! Fight for the Bearcats!" She recovered, and said she learned God does not care what words we use in prayer. He only cares what we mean.

Near the end of the day, I mentioned that Christian Scientists have practiced spiritual healing for more than a century. Others nodded recognition. They remembered reading the Monitor in college, but some assumed Christian Science, like the Shakers, no longer existed. I was happy to correct the mistake, which was easily explained by the large number of Christian Science branch churches in Indiana that disbanded for lack of members. Most edifices were converted to new uses. In Huntington, for example, the former Christian Science church is now the Dan Quayle Vice-Presidential Museum, where you can see his law school diploma, which was famously chewed by the family dog.

But some Hoosier Christian Science churches continued to bless their community, even after they closed. The congregation in Boonville disbanded in 1995, and after the edifice was sold and all debts paid, they voted to use most of their remaining funds to establish an irrevocable trust at Boonville People's Trust and Savings Bank. The trust was administered by the bank president, who eventually became the only surviving church member. Interest from the trust is still used each year to award grants to non-profit organizations within Warrick County that uphold the church's values through community service. One year, for example, $53,000 was awarded, including $2,0000 to a soup kitchen, $6,000 to the Tri-State Food Bank, and $5,000 to the Warrick County Council on Aging. During the first 19 years, local agencies received $1.4 million from the trust, and the church is remembered fondly.

Lesser known but equally loving were a small handful of Christian Scientists who worshipped in rural Bremen, Indiana, from 1941 until they disbanded in 1953. Services were held in the home of two members, Mr. and Mrs. William E. Walter. During all those years, the town library was crammed into a room in the Town Hall. More space was needed, and a citizen committee was formed to explore possibilities for growth. Donations were modest until Mrs. Walter contributed $15,000 in 1954 to help the committee acquire her now-vacant home. During the fund-drive, Anita Morland, wife of school superintendent John Morland, wrote an essay for the Bremen Enquirer called "I Am the Library." It began, "I am the library. Listen to my words, America, for now I speak. My cornerstone has been laid by the great thinkers of all ages of men. My walls are sturdy protection from all the shackles of which man has conceived—spiritual as well as physical."

Mrs. Walter found the article so eloquent that she sent a copy to the editor of the Christian Science Monitor. When he reprinted it on July 23, 1955, Monitor readers across the nation learned about Bremen and its dream of a new library. Local residents increased their donations, and a modest library was soon ready to open. Everyone agreed it should be called the W.E. Walter Memorial Library. The structure has expanded since then, but still stands on the corner where Christian Scientists worshipped faithfully for a dozen years, and loved their community.

As I drove thousands of miles across Indiana, meeting face-to-face with as many legislators and editors as possible, I discovered the Manager of Committees on Publication was correct. None had ever spoken with a Christian Scientist before, except perhaps an elderly relative. Some newsrooms treated me like a visiting dignitary, snapping my photo for tomorrow's paper. Other editors gladly let me write an article about Christian Science for their religion page. After I told one editor that Christian Science does not prohibit any form of health care, she took my hand in both of hers and thanked me. "Before I came to meet you," she said, "my assistant editor warned me, 'those are the people who don't believe in doctors.'" She was very relieved.

No matter how much one enjoys his work, one aspect is always loved best, and my favorite part of Committee work was an annual statewide workshop hosted by the centrally located church in Carmel, Indiana. A secret agenda at each workshop was to help members from tiny, distant churches feel less scattered and more gathered. Sometimes the Carmel church was nearly full on workshop day as we heard inspiring guest speakers from the Manager's office in Boston. Those who attended cherished warm fellowship, and took home fresh ideas to share with fellow members. One Hoosier Christian Scientist later wrote, "We were a small but dedicated remnant, but before you took the Committee job and ran with it, we were demoralized. Your visits, photos, contacts with news people, meetings and jolly encouragement have really sparked us up."

After I served three busy years as Committee for Indiana, Evelyn and I welcomed a grandson, and his parents lived in Raleigh, North Carolina. So we could spend more time with him, I resigned and we prepared to move. A few weeks before our home sold, my cell phone rang as I looked at books in the local library. It was the Manager of Committees on Publication in Boston with an unexpected question. Would I be willing, if invited by proper officials, to serve next year as Committee for North Carolina? As far as I knew, no other Committee had ever served in two states with no interval between them. The opportunity was irresistible and I gratefully agreed. It would be a gratifying occupation to enhance the enjoyment we planned to have with our family.

19

Back to the public practice of Christian Science

North Carolina is a rich thread in the tapestry of Christian Science history. Mary Baker Eddy, who later founded the denomination, was living in Wilmington, North Carolina, with her first husband, George Washington Glover, when he died of yellow fever in 1844. After the funeral, Glover's fellow Free Masons assisted his grieving widow back to her parents' home in New Hampshire.

Many years later, when Mrs. Eddy described Glover's tragic death in her autobiography, "Retrospection and Introspection," a critic disputed her account by claiming her husband was never a Free Mason. Some Masonic records were destroyed during the Civil War, leaving Glover's true status in doubt, until Mary Hatch Harrison, one of the first Christian Scientists in North Carolina, conducted extensive research and proved Mrs. Eddy's account correct.

Christian Science came to North Carolina in 1894 when Harrison, of New Bern, was reportedly healed of paralysis by studying the Bible and Mrs. Eddy's writings. She began holding services in her home, and in 1902 a church was organized with 18 members.

Mrs. Eddy was so grateful to Harrison for verifying the true Masonic status of her late husband that she participated in establishing the church in New Bern. She donated a granite block for the cornerstone and sent copies of all her writings to be placed in the stone, as well as a gift of $3,000 for the building fund. She also selected the four inscriptions seen on the interior walls of the church. The Classical Revival-style edifice, dedicated free from debt in 1907, was the first Christian Science church built in North Carolina, and remains active today.

Meanwhile, in 1907, seven Christian Scientists began conducting services in Asheville, and their church was completed in 1912. Elizabeth Earl Jones was among the charter members. She and Harrison each served as early Committees on Publication for North Carolina. Their pioneering work is described near the end of Mrs. Eddy's book, "The First Church of Christ, Scientist and Miscellany."

By the time I arrived from Indiana, Harrison and Jones were not the only dedicated North Carolina Committees whose shoes waited to be filled. Another previous Committee was superstar bandleader Kay Kyser, president of the "Kollege of Musical Knowledge."

Kyser studied Christian Science while in show business before and after World War II. Beginning in 1956, he served 14 years as Committee on Publication for North Carolina. During those years he became a practitioner listed in the Christian Science Journal, and then a teacher authorized to instruct others in the faith. Following his years as Committee, he worked for The Mother Church in Boston, serving as its president in 1983.

My term as North Carolina Committee was shorter and less historic than Harrison's or Jones' or Kyser's, but the welcome I received from church members was very warm. Curious why a Hoosier from the Midwest was appointed to be their media and legislative liaison, most congregations in the state, including Wilmington, New Bern and Asheville, invited me to speak after a worship service on Sunday. My goal then, as in Indiana, was to help everyone feel less scattered and more gathered, and some familiar faces appeared along the way. Nearly half the members of one small church had gone to Camp Elektor as children and brought photos to prove it. The Reading Room librarian at another church had worked with me at the Christian Science Monitor. But the most surprising reunion came after I spoke at the Christian

Science church in Charlotte. "You don't remember me, do you?" asked a sweet lady. I confessed I didn't, and then she gave a hint. "We went to the high school senior prom together in Media, Pennsylvania." She and I hadn't met since then, but we still shared the memory of that wonderful night.

The state legislature adjourned before I arrived in Raleigh, and did not reconvene during my year as Committee. Without any legislative concerns, I had ample time to meet editors in many newsrooms across the state face-to-face. During months of travel, I learned of a church member who was eminently qualified for the work I was doing. A skilled writer, she was familiar with the state legislature and knew some lawmakers. Most importantly, she was a team player who lived Christian Science and would humbly follow directions received from the Manager in Boston. State Committees are appointed annually, and she was busy with other obligations when I arrived in North Carolina, but as the year progressed she became more available, so I declined re-appointment and was grateful when she was appointed to fill the vacancy. In my heart, I felt a call to once again enter the full-time healing practice of Christian Science.

Requirements to advertise in the Christian Science Journal as a practitioner have varied slightly over the decades. When I first applied, I had to submit letters from three patients who had been healed by my prayers within the past year, and only two could be church members. When I reapplied several years later, letters were required from three patients who had been healed by my prayers during the past five years, and all could be church members. This bar seemed a bit lower, but I assumed it would take a year to obtain such letters. God apparently felt otherwise.

Within six weeks, patients from Florida, Indiana and North Carolina provided the needed letters, which I forwarded to the Journal. A few weeks later an envelope arrived from the trustees of the Christian Science Publishing Society. They wrote, "We're delighted to inform you that your application to reinsert your advertising card in the Christian Science Journal has been accepted. This step reflects your continued devotion and willingness to advertise as a fully available public Christian Science practitioner."

Serving as Committee on Publication for Indiana and North Carolina taught me something about prevailing prayer. In a verse from of his many poems, my former Sunday school teacher, Peter Henniker-Heaton, put it this way:

He who would take his ship to sea
must loose the cable from the quay,
must raise the heavy anchor-chain
from the sea-bed where it has lain;
but let him not forget to cut
the silken threads of Lilliput."

"Jubilee and Other Poems," (E.D. Abbot & Co., Boston, 1971, p. 24)

The silken threads of Lilliput symbolize different things to different people. For me, they are narrow, almost invisible temptations to believe my prayer heals others because of my personal goodness or deep study or steady resolve. These human virtues, even when cloaked in piety, seldom heal the sick. For me, healings happen when I refuse to accept the illusion calling itself a "patient," when I refuse to see anyone as a mortal—good or bad, sick or well, alive or dead. Mrs. Eddy taught that God's law is in three words, "I am All." Obeying this law lifts the burden of personal responsibility from my shoulders, and some healings are quicker than expected. Take Margaret, for example. I've changed her name, but her story is true.

When Margaret was 12, she was playing basketball and the girl who was guarding her accidentally tripped her, causing her to fall. Margaret finished the game holding back tears because her knee was turning black and blue and her calf muscle hurt. Three days later, she needed to play goalie in a soccer game, so her parents wrapped her leg carefully. She was eager to play, but during the game another player accidentally kicked her injured calf muscle, and she came off the field in tears. She'd been using crutches since the basketball injury, and now this. She felt discouraged by lack of progress, and couldn't control her fear, so, in her own words: "I emailed Dave Horn for practitioner help. My knee was black and blue. He reminded me that God is always in control, and that I can't be hurt by expressing Godlike qualities. The next morning when I woke up, my knee was all healed! I am so thankful."

Margaret neglected to say that her email to me was very cryptic, like a text message. She asked for prayerful support but never hinted why it was needed. Sometimes such ignorance benefits a practitioner. By removing the temptation to pray for a bruised knee, it turns attention to the eternal fact of God's allness.

After answering Margaret's email, I took the advice I'd given Sunday School pupils in the past, and endeavored to "think as God thinks." It wasn't hard to see her through His eyes—unfallen, painless and spiritual, perfect in every way. I went to sleep that night convinced this is Margaret's actual condition, now and always. When she called the next day to tell about her healing, I was as thankful as she was.

During the next year, God's allness was apparent in other healings. A farmer from Indiana wrote, "My healing is complete. I can lift 50 pound bags of feed again, and carry them into the barn." A young mother who had been suffering with a toothache wrote, "It's been a long time since I've had such a complete healing. I felt I had a breakthrough with not just studying God's truth, but putting it into action." And a Sunday school pupil from North Carolina added, "This message is a gratitude note for your friendly support and your teachings. They have helped me throughout my life so far."

But what if God was less than All? What if He was not all loving and omnipotent? These questions demanded answers when distressing symptoms sent me to the Emergency Room at Rex Hospital, where I was diagnosed with acute heart failure.

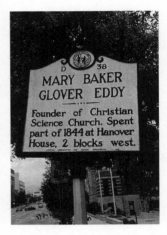

This marker stands on 3rd Street near Market Street in Wilmington, NC. While living in the city, newlyweds Mr. and Mrs. George Washington Glover worshipped at St. James Episcopal church on S. 3rd St. Here Mrs. Eddy's first husband is buried in the church yard.

Mrs. Eddy sent $3,000 to help finance construction of this edifice in New Bern. It was the first branch of The Mother Church in North Carolina.

Mrs. Eddy personally selected verses to be engraved on interior walls of the church.

❧20

The voice of God

*T*he Christian Science church does not prohibit any form of health care, nor do Christian Scientists regard medicine as sinful. If they rely on prayer to heal illness, it's usually because prayer cured them in the past. When I was a child, my life was saved through the same type of prevailing prayer that later healed me at summer camp and in the Navy, and guided me to true companionship. I had trusted my health to God for more than 60 years when doctors in the emergency room attached three IV's to my arms, taped a heart monitor to my chest, and rushed me to the Cardio Intensive Care Unit (ICU), where a computer monitored my condition and nurses checked my status every 30 minutes.

Mary Baker Eddy's advice was helpful to me that day. In a sermon called "Christian Healing" she wrote, "If you employ a medical practitioner, be sure he is a learned man and skillful; never trust yourself in the hands of a quack." Then she explained why. "In proportion as a physician is enlightened and liberal he is equipped with Truth, and his efforts are salutary…"

I was reminded of this when the cardiologist assigned to me entered the room and introduced himself. Dr. J said all my "vital signs" were falling and my heart had lost 90% of its strength. He said I had a 50-50 chance of survival at best, and should remain quiet and obey all instructions carefully.

He struck me as a sincere young man with my best interest in mind. He was not dramatic or frightening. Only later did I learn his premed work was done at Harvard and he was currently President of the North Carolina chapter of the American College of Cardiology. He had been a professor of Cardiology and Radiology at Duke University, where he was recognized for excellence in teaching. Nationally, he worked with thousands of colleagues across the country to organize emergency cardiac care in New York City, Houston, Atlanta, St. Louis and Philadelphia, and he was currently working with 119 hospitals and 500 emergency medical services to coordinate cardiac arrest care, while he and his wife raised two teenagers. He also owned a boat, but had very little time to enjoy it.

During our first meeting, Dr. J introduced me to his medical assistant, Meaghan, one of the nicest people in the world. When you're near the end of life, niceness matters, and she was kindness personified. Dr. J. saw me briefly once each day, but Meaghan was never in a hurry. She'd sit smiling beside my bed, listen to all my concerns and answer my questions honestly. Sometimes she'd stay 15 minutes, which is a very long time in the ICU.

One day I asked her frankly, "If I survive, how long should it take me to feel well again?" She could have said, "Your heart is so weak that it's impossible to know what will happen," but instead she said, "Well, that depends. Everyone is different. We can't predict how long your recovery will take because you're special." From that moment on, I didn't feel terminal. I felt special.

Even with her encouragement, it was difficult to remain hopeful, especially at night when the only light in my room was a glowing computer screen. The bed was not comfortable and I could not roll over. I could not even get out of bed without ringing first for a nurse. On the third night, as I lay in the dark, I began to wonder if maybe my life had been long enough. I felt I had no choices left, nobody in the hospital really knew me, and God seemed far away. Why struggle on? With these sad thoughts I drifted into a fitful sleep.

Then, sometime later, I was suddenly awakened by a very bright light. The light was so bright that my room looked beautiful. I glanced at the drapes on the windows, and they appeared gorgeous. Peering around, I said "Wow!" and then heard a voice as clearly as if someone else was in the room with me. It said, "I am here now, and I know you." Quickly I grabbed a pad and pencil and wrote down the words, to prove I was not dreaming. Then I lay back again, feeling pure happiness as darkness returned. To me, it was the voice of God. I could hardly believe God cared enough to actually remind me of His ever-presence, and promise that even here in the ICU, He still knew me. What more could anyone ask? This was as good as it gets.

As I lay joyfully in the dark, a new idea came to mind. Even if I could not choose to roll over or get out of bed without permission, I still had one choice left in life. I could choose to be thankful. I decided to make that my choice, and from then on, no matter what uncomfortable or embarrassing things I was asked to do, I thanked the staff sincerely for their help. It made their days easier, and I felt better too.

That night, after the bright light faded, two nurses routinely checked my room. Seeing me awake, they asked how I was. "Never better!" I said honestly, which brought both nurses to my bed. "Who are you, really?" they asked in the dim light from the corridor. I said I was a Christian Scientist, and knew God cares for all his children, including everyone in the hospital that night, because He told me.

Both nurses were suddenly interested and interrupted their schedule to chat a few minutes. One explained how she prays each day before coming to work, asking God to help her comfort her patients on the night shift. By the time they left, we all agreed God was in the room, and they resumed their rounds with fresh inspiration.

After three days, my "vital signs" had stabilized and I was transferred to a private room in the main hospital. Meaghan still came to see me every day, and Dr. J, who came every few days, admitted he was "cautiously optimistic."

A week later, he authorized my release from the hospital.

Home care specialists visited our home several times each week, and I would measure my pulse and blood pressure on a device which transmitted this data back to the hospital. I had lost so much weight that I looked like a refugee, but Dr. J gave me strict instructions. "What you need most now is to enjoy life, so that your heart can heal. Just enjoy life."

My stepdaughters made homecoming as sweet as possible. One brought delicious food while the other gave me a hug and a much needed haircut. And Evelyn's 24/7 care was tireless. A life-long student of Christian Science, she knew nothing about medical nursing, but she monitored my medicines, prepared my delicious low-salt meals and even gave me shots when necessary. Some fellow members at our Christian Science church delivered flowers and more than a dozen tasty homemade dinners, while others accompanied us to the hospital for weekly check-ups, helping Evelyn push my wheelchair down the long corridors.

As I rested at home, I pondered Dr. J's reminder to "enjoy life." Why was this so important? I had no problem getting through life, but seldom felt happy about it. I realized with regret that my default attitude was criticism, not joy, and I asked God to show me reasons for pure happiness. There was no overnight change, but gradually I began to "feel" the love others felt for me, and return it in ways that made them happy. Doing this made me joyful too.

After three months, I could walk with a cane and returned to the hospital for an echocardiogram which let me see my heart as a new mother sees her unborn baby. Minutes later Dr. J came to the room, and when he saw the video, he was obviously surprised.

"When you came to us, you had the weakest heart I've ever seen that was still beating," he admitted. "But look at it now. The clot is gone. Your heart is healthy. In my experience, this is almost a miracle." Then, jokingly, he added, "Don't buy any more lottery tickets. You've used up all your luck."

After receiving this good news, I told him about the voice I heard in the ICU that said, "I am here now, and I know you." He encouraged me to always listen for that voice and obey it. "It restored your hope," he explained. "Research has shown that heart patients who give up hope never survive."

He said the medicine I was prescribed could not actually heal my heart, any more than a splint can heal a broken bone. It only helps makes healing possible. Other factors determine if a heart will heal, which is why he urged me so strongly to "enjoy life."

I believe the choice to be thankful, which I made in the ICU, also helped the healing process, and ever since then, I've cherished these words from an old gospel hymn. "Our Father's love is never complete 'til it reaches the hearts that fail."

Following my recovery, I asked God if I could be useful to him from home. Then I listened, and a very strange thought came immediately to mind. Start a blog called "Crumbs of Comfort" to discover, share and archive evidence of divine fingerprints on the lives of everyday folks of all faiths. I'd never read a blog and had no idea how to begin, but within an hour it was up and running. Since it began in August, 2014, "Crumbs of Comfort" (comfortcrumb.blogspot.com) has been updated daily and enjoyed over 18,000 page visits from readers in a dozen nations. It's also featured on the Web sites of four newspapers in the United States. Some readers who find evidence of God's fingerprints in their local media forward these stories to me as "possible crumbs" and I gratefully post them.

On the day in 1970 when my father died, mother and I cleaned out his bedroom and found a Christian Science Hymnal on his desk, laying open to page 234, the last hymn he read before passing away. The words were written by Washington Gladden, a journalist-turned-minister during America's Gilded Age (1870-1914), and he first published them in 1879.

Dad never claimed to be perfect, and in the greenness of youth I saw his shortcomings vividly. He never hugged me or said he loved me, but in memory's halo I've realized how hard he worked for my success, and why this hymn was his heartfelt prayer and benediction. It's also mine.

> "O Master, let me walk with thee
> In lowly paths of service free;
> Tell me thy secret; help me bear
> The strain of toil, the fret of care.
>
> In hope that sends a shining ray
> Far down the future's broadening way;
> In peace that God alone can give,
> With thee, O Master, let me live."